Beast on Wall Street

How Stock Volatility Devours Our Wealth

Robert A. Haugen

Professor of Finance, University of California, Irvine

Prentice Hall
Upper Saddle River, New Jersey 07458

Acquisitions Editor:	Paul Donnelly
Editorial Assistant:	Jodi Hirsh
Editorial Director:	James C. Boyd
Marketing Manager:	Patrick Lynch
Production Editor:	Evyan Jengo
Permissions Coordinator:	Monica Stipanov
Managing Editor:	Dee Josephson
Manufacturing Buyer:	Diane Peirano
Manufacturing Supervisor:	Arnold Vila
Manufacturing Manager:	Vincent Scelta
Cover Design:	Bruce Kenselaar
Cover Photo:	Mark Newman/Photo Network
Composition:	Omegatype Topography, Inc.

 Copyright © 1999 by Prentice-Hall, Inc.

A Simon & Schuster Company

Upper Saddle River, New Jersey 07458

Library of Congress Cataloging-in-Publication Data
Haugen, Robert A.
    Beast on Wall Street : how stock volatility devours our wealth /
by Robert A. Haugen.
        p.   cm.
    Includes bibliographical references (p.   ).
    ISBN 0-13-080078-3 (pbk.)
    1. Stocks—Prices—United States.   I. Title.
HG4915.H378   1998
332.63'222'0973—dc21   98-14534
                                                                 CIP

Prentice-Hall International (UK) Limited, London
Prentice-Hall of Australia Pty. Limited, Sydney
Prentice-Hall Canada, Inc., Toronto
Prentice-Hall Hispanoamericana, S.A., Mexico
Prentice-Hall of India Private Limited, New Delhi
Prentice-Hall of Japan, Inc., Tokyo
Simon & Schuster Asia Pte. Ltd., Singapore
Editora Prentice-Hall do Brasil, Ltda., Rio de Janeiro

Printed in the United States of America

10 9 8 7 6 5 4 3 2 1

This book is dedicated to the real Tiffany Meyer

Additional Prentice Hall titles by Robert Haugen:

- Modern Investment Theory, Fourth Edition, 1997
- The New Finance, Second Edition, 1999
- The Inefficient Market, 1999

Visit Robert Haugen's Web site at:
http://www.bobhaugen.com

Contents

Preface: Beware, THE BEAST Is a Bear

Sometimes we don't realize that something is very, very wrong. We don't realize because, in our experience, even in history, it has *always* been wrong. Although the consequences of the flaw are enormous, we don't realize what we are dealing with; because we always carry the burden, we never truly feel its weight.

This book is about such a burden. Surprisingly, it resides in the *stock exchange*. Free of its weight, the risk of investing in stock might be a tenth of what it has been. Stock prices might be many times higher than they are today. The cost of equity capital might be reduced by a conservative two-thirds. Corporations might have invested much more, and it is likely that real economic growth in this country, and in others, would have been much greater than it has been throughout our history.

Astonishingly, we can easily cast the terrible burden away. Simply by changing the rules under which shares are exchanged.

In fact, we *are* changing the rules. They are *evolving*. But, unfortunately, they are evolving in *the wrong direction*. Moving us toward higher stock volatility, a higher cost of capital, reduced investment, and slower economic growth. As the rules continue to evolve, we may eventually feel the weight of the burden increasing and finally recognize the enormous economic destruction wrought by THE BEAST.

ACKNOWLEDGMENTS

I have benefited from discussions with Peter Bernstein, Bill Conners, Greg Kipnis, Roger Johnson, Philippe Jorion, Dennis Logue, Harry Markowitz, Robert Shiller, Neal Stoughton, Joe Williams, and especially Charles Cuny. I would also like to thank Valeska Wolf for processing the manuscript.

Robert A. Haugen
University of California, Irvine

Introduction

How to get you to read the rest of this book?

What can I say? First of all, reading this book won't take much time or effort. It's only about 150 pages long. And it's got some excitement. Plenty of intrigue. Seven mysteries. Count them—seven! All solved too. And, believe it or not, the body count is nearly as high as in an average Schwarzenegger movie. You'll learn some really interesting things along the way, like: "What's the principal driver behind stock prices?" And the next time the stock market comes crashing down, you'll know why.

You'll also learn about the connecting link between a luncheon speech given on September 6, 1929, in New York City and the sequence of events leading through the Great Depression into World War II!

And when you hear a "suit" talk knowingly about the Efficient Markets Hypothesis, you'll be able to chuckle.

The Efficient Markets Hypothesis? What's that?

That's something they thought up in business schools in the early 1960s. It was designed to forever lift finance professors a level above the professionals working on Wall Street.

The Wall Street types are out there trying very hard. Combing through financial reports and charts. Talking to investment relations officers. Trying to get an edge. Trying to find a bargain. Trying to find an undervalued stock.

There are thousands of these guys.

According to the Efficient Markets Hypothesis, they're like a band of treasure hunters looking for pocket change with metal detectors.

The treasure's all but gone. The band of professional investors has done their job *too* well. Supposedly, there aren't any bargains left!

In selling short the bad (overpriced) stocks and buying the good (underpriced) stocks, they have pushed all stocks to the point where their prices *always* reflect *everything* that is relevant and knowable about the companies behind them.

Really.

Always. And *everything.*

When the stock market reaches this remarkable state, the only information that prices don't reflect is new information that has not yet been received and cannot be predicted.

Everything that's predictable at all is already accurately reflected in stock prices. Only completely unpredictable things aren't.

Completely unpredictable events come in randomly. The efficient stock market responds to these events instantly and accurately. Changes in stock prices are then based pretty much on the receipt of these unpredictable events. Thus, changes in stock prices will be random, too. That's why the Efficient Markets Hypothesis is sometimes called the *Random Walk Hypothesis.*

You see, *it's convenient being a level above the professionals on Wall Street.*

Student: "Professor Smith. I have been told that there are many technical chartists in the investment community. Can you teach me how to forecast future stock prices based on the patterns in past stock prices?"

Professor Smith (who simply knows nothing about charting): "Haven't you been paying attention? Stock prices move randomly. You simply can't forecast future stock prices by looking at past stock prices. Chartists are all idiots!"

Student: "I think I understand, Professor Smith. But what about the other guys? The analysts who don't chart base their analysis on fundamentals. They do things like forecast earnings-per-share. Can you teach me how to forecast earnings-per-share?"

Professor Smith (who has never made an earnings forecast in his life): "Don't you remember what I told you yesterday? Stock prices already reflect the best possible forecasts of earnings-per-share. Those fundamental analysts, who are trying to outfox the market, are simply wasting their time!"

Student: "Okay, Professor. Now I think I'm beginning to get the picture. But there's another group of professionals called portfolio managers. These people take the recommendations of security analysts and decide how much to invest in each stock so that risk is controlled and "bets" are diversified over sectors, industries, and individual stocks. Could you show us how to do *that?*"

Professor Smith (who has never managed a portfolio in his life): "Listen, in the efficient market that's really not a problem. We know from the Capital Asset Pricing Model that the market index has the lowest risk given its expected return. So you simply spread your investments between the index and risk-free Treasury Bills to achieve the level of risk that you want."

Student: "Boy, the investment business is really simple. But what if I want to become a pension officer? Could you show me how to evaluate the skills of money managers, so I can pick the best money managers for my fund?"

Professor Smith (who has never talked to or evaluated a money manager in his life): "Don't worry about that. In the efficient market all managers have the same skill at beating the market—none."

Student: "Gee, if it's all that simple, then why do I need this class?"

That is an interesting question indeed!

You see, professors, who are trained only in financial economics have a vested interest in the Efficient Markets Hypothesis. They can act as though they are training students to become professional investors without really training them to do anything at all. And that's quite fortunate for the professors, who for the most part, *haven't the necessary skills to train students in the craft of investment management!*

But, given the Efficient Markets Hypothesis, the professors can arrogantly stand one level above the investment professionals. The professionals may *think* they know what's going on, but only the professors can see the BIG picture.

That's why they cling to their hypothesis with such great zeal!

However, they might ask themselves the following question: "If, over the last few decades, few have been trained in the craft of investing in their MBA finance classes, *who in blazes is supposed to be making the market so efficient?*"

The sorry truth is that those who believe in the Efficient Markets Hypothesis are *dead wrong.*

First of all, changes in stock prices are not random at all. There are short-term reversal patterns in stock prices. If a stock has done well in the last month or two, it will likely underperform in the future.[1] There is also evidence of inertia in the intermediate term. If a stock has outperformed in the last 6 to 12 months it will likely outperform in the future as well.[2] Finally, there are reversal patterns over the long term. If a stock has outperformed in the last 3 to 5 years, it will tend to underperform in the future.[3]

In addition, there are strong seasonal patterns in stock returns. The research findings on several of the seasonal features in stock returns are surveyed and explained in a book I co-authored called *The Incredible January Effect.*[4]

Moreover, stock prices do not accurately reflect all that is knowable. The market is both imprecise and biased in its pricing. *Bias* is the topic of my book, *The New Finance: The Case Against Efficient Markets.*[5] *Imprecision* will be covered in my next book, *The Inefficient Stock Market—What Pays Off and Why.*

This book is about *noise*—discordant movements in stock prices. Discordance, which creates even more volatility in stock returns. *Too much volatility.* Most of the noise comes from the market reacting to *its own pricing behaviors.* And noise constitutes the *lion's share* of the market's volatility!

Because the focus of this book is stock volatility, it's probably a good idea to start by explaining just what volatility is.

An example will help. Suppose we follow a stock for four years and find that it produces the following four returns, –10%, 0%, 20%, and 30%, for an average of 10%. Note that, although the average is 10%, the return in each year deviates from the average. The deviations are –20%, –10%, +10%, and +20%, respectively. Now square the deviations to obtain 400%, 100%, 100%, and 400%, for an average of *250%.*[6] This is the *variance* of the four returns. If we take the square root of the variance, we get the standard deviation, which is roughly 16%. *This is what we refer to as volatility.*

Normally, roughly two-thirds of the annual returns will fall within one standard deviation from the average. So, if this sequence is representative, we can expect that two-thirds of its annual returns will fall between –6% and 26%.

The volatility of the market's returns can be taken as a measure of risk. It's a measure of how rough the stock-market ride is on our way to a prosperous retirement. As we shall see, the road isn't uniformly paved. It gets smoother and then suddenly rougher. Volatility is very unstable.

And I think you will find the story behind that instability to be a particularly fascinating one.

The book is divided into three parts. Part I presents seven mysteries, or anomalies, that have been found by academic research into stock market behavior. As it turns out, all seven mysteries can be solved based on the statements that preceded this paragraph. By solving the seven mysteries, a case is made for the fact that (a) stock volatility is much too big, (b) the cost of equity capital is much too high, and (c) investment spending and economic growth have been, are, and should continue to be much too low.

The mysteries are partially synthesized within a short story that constitutes Part II.

Part III completes the synthesis and discusses the implications of the findings.

Please keep reading.

Robert A. Haugen
University of California, Irvine

Notes

1. N. Jegadeesh, 1993, "Evidence of Predictable Behavior of Security Returns," *Journal of Finance,* pp. 881–898.
2. N. Jegadeesh, and S. Titman, 1993, "Returns to Buying Winners and Selling Losers," *Journal of Finance,* pp. 65–91.
3. W. De Bondt, and R. Thaler, 1985, "Does the Stock Market Over-react?" *Journal of Finance,* pp. 793–808.
4. R. Haugen, and J. Lakonishok, *The Incredible January Effect,* (Dow Jones-Irwine, Homewood, IL, 1986)
5. R. Haugen, 1995, *The New Finance: The Case Against Efficient Markets,* (Prentice Hall, Upper Saddle River, NJ)
6. Normally, with a small sample like this, we would compute the average by dividing by the number of years less 1.00 to obtain an unbiased estimate of the variance.

PART I

The Seven Mysteries of the Stock Market

THE FIRST MYSTERY: STOCK PRICES ARE TOO VOLATILE

How Volatile Is *Too* Volatile?

Anyone who has paid any attention at all to the stock market knows that when you invest in stocks, you're likely in for a wild ride. The difference between investing in stocks and, say, investing in Treasury Bills is akin to the difference between the Rocket Coaster and the merry-go-round at your local amusement park.

But what does it mean to say that stocks are *too* volatile?

The fundamental support for the market price of any investment is the future cash flows that the investor expects to receive. In the case of a bond, these are the semiannual interest payments and the principal payment received at maturity. In the case of a stock, the cash flows are dividends.

If dividends are the fundamental basis of stock prices, it follows that, over the long term, the volatility of stock prices should be *consistent* with the volatility of dividends.

But they are not. The evidence points to the conclusion that the volatility of stock prices is much too high relative to variability in the dividend stream.

To understand clearly why the evidence points to this conclusion, we must first understand some basic concepts.

The Perfect Foresight Price

The first is called the *Perfect Foresight Price*. This is the price that God would agree is the fair value for the stock.

God knows what the future (inflation-adjusted) dividend payments are going to be for the stock. God also knows what real (inflation-adjusted) interest rates are going to be.

Once we've got a long history of stock dividend payments, we can go back and get a pretty good estimate of what God's price would have been in the past.

1

If we go back 50 years, we discount the actual dividend payments paid over the next 50 years by the interest, or discount, rates that prevailed when each dividend was paid.

Consider God's price at the start of the 50 years. In the first year suppose that the inflation-adjusted first and second quarter's dividends are both $1.00. Suppose also that the current quarterly, risk-adjusted real interest rate is 1% and the quarterly rate that will prevail next quarter is 2%. The present value of the first dividend is $.99 = ($1.00/(1.01)) and the present value of the second is $.97 = ($1.00/(1.01)(1.02)).

If you think about it, you will realize that *the Perfect Foresight Price is not constant through time.*

God may not see a smooth or level dividend stream coming. As we move from one point in the past to another, the Perfect Foresight Price rises with an increase in the size of the near-term dividend payments relative to the payments received at the point in time when the Perfect Foresight Price was first calculated.

For example, consider the pattern of quarterly dividend payments depicted in Figure 1.1. In this hypothetical economy, we go from boom to bust every other year. In boom years, the quarterly dividend is $2.00. In busts, it falls to $1.00.

Now consider God's price as we move along in time from points A to B to C. The Perfect Foresight Price goes up in moving from A to B, because, at B, the next boom is upon us, while at A, it is a full year off. Assuming the rate of discount doesn't change over time, the present value of future dividends is larger

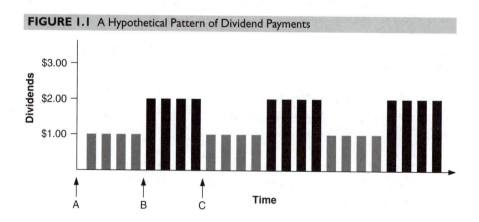

FIGURE 1.1 A Hypothetical Pattern of Dividend Payments

at *B*. God's price goes up. For similar reasons, it falls back as we go from *B* to *C*. At *C*, the next boom is, once again, a full year off.

Holding everything else constant, it should also be true that, as we move retrospectively into a period in which quarterly interest rates will be relatively low for a while, the Perfect Foresight Price will tend to increase. This is because the near-term dividends, which are most important to the present value, are being discounted at lower rates.

The Efficient Market Relationship between the Volatilities of the Perfect Foresight Price and the Market Price

If the market is efficient, what should the relationship be between the volatility of the Perfect Forecast Price and the volatility of the actual market price for the stock or stocks?

In Figure 1.2a, we plot changes in the Perfect Forecast Price on the vertical axis and changes in the actual market price on the horizontal. Each point shows the relationship between the two changes during a particular period of time.

The market of Figure 1.2a is overreactive.

Changes in the Perfect Foresight Price induce changes in the actual market price that are many times larger. For example, in Figure 1.2a, as we move into a period where near-term dividends are relatively large (like the periods

FIGURE 1.2a Relationship between Changes in Perfect Forecast Price and Changes in Market Price in an Overreactive Market

just before a boom in Figure 1.1), the Perfect Foresight Price rises, as it does at point *A*. But the corresponding increase in the market price, plotted horizontally, is four times as large. Based on the points in Figure 1.2a, we see that this market reacts in an exaggerated fashion to changes in the Perfect Forecast Price. When it goes up, market prices go up further. When it goes down, prices go down further.

In the context of Figure 1.1, the market price would move up and down from boom to bust by more than the changes occurring in the Perfect Foresight Price.

An efficient-markets person would say that smart investors would soon catch on to the overreactions in stock prices. They would sell into big advances in stock prices and buy into big declines.

If the market eventually corrected its tendency to overreact, the relationship between changes in the two prices would look like that in Figure 1.2b. Here, *on average,* changes in the two prices tend to be equal. The market doesn't get it right every time, but it gets it right *on average.*

We have drawn a line of best fit[1] through the scatter of Figure 1.2b. In the unbiased and efficient market of Figure 1.2b, the slope of this line is equal to 1.00. When the market reaches this state of efficiency in pricing, it can be shown that, if the market price and the Perfect Foresight Price are perfectly correlated, their *variances* (volatility squared) must be equal to each other. If the two prices are not perfectly correlated, the efficient market ratio of the Perfect Foresight variance to the actual market variance must be, at most, equal to the coefficient of correlation between the two prices.[2]

FIGURE 1.2b Relationship in an Efficient Market

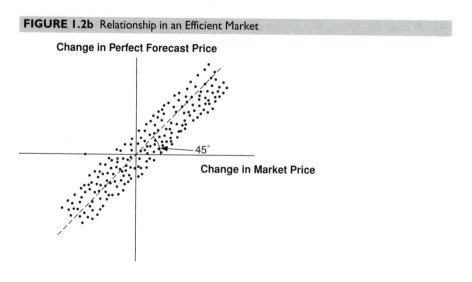

Change in Perfect Forecast Price

45°

Change in Market Price

Because the maximum possible value for the correlation between the market and perfect foresight prices is 1.00, we now know that, *in an efficient market, the volatility of actual market prices must be less than or at most equal to the volatility of the Perfect Foresight Price.*

The Actual Relationship between the Market Price and the Current Forecast Price

Now let's look at the *actual* relationship between the volatility of stock market prices and the volatility of estimates of the Perfect Foresight Price.

Figure 1.3 shows a plot constructed by a professor named Robert Shiller.[3] In the figure, Shiller plots (as the solid line) the time series of the ratio of (a) the inflation-adjusted value of the Standard and Poor's 500 Stock Index and (b) the 30-year moving average of inflation-adjusted earnings-per-share for the index.

Note that it is highly volatile.

Next, Shiller estimates the time series of Perfect Foresight Prices. He uses the equation for the Perfect Forecast Price, discounting inflation-adjusted dividends paid by the stocks in the index (from each point in time forward) by quarterly interest rates that are assumed to be constant and equal to approximately 2% each.[4] The estimates of the Perfect Forecast Prices are also divided by the 30-year moving-average earnings numbers, and the ratio is plotted as the broken line.

The efficient market limit to the market's variance is grossly violated.

FIGURE 1.3 Market Price and Perfect Forecast Price: Constant Discount Rates

Source: Shiller, Robert, *Market Volatility,* The MIT Press, Cambridge, MA, 1990, p. 78.

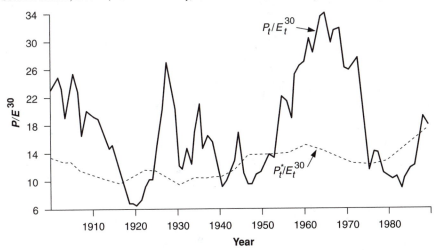

The market's variance is apparently not only not smaller than the variance of Shiller's Perfect Foresight Price; it is—based on this initial look—much, much larger.

Knowing that interest rates are not constant over time, Shiller now uses the actual series of commercial paper rates that were in effect over the time-series.[5] He adds a constant risk premium to the commercial paper rates to obtain the quarterly discount rates used in the equation for the Perfect Foresight Price.[6]

Figure 1.4 shows the new series of Perfect Foresight Prices superimposed on the actual stock price series. The volatility of the actual series is still 44% *greater* than the volatility of the Perfect Foresight Price. Moreover, the correlation between the two series is only .047, indicating a gross violation of the level of price volatility consistent with the Efficient Markets Hypothesis.

Shiller's work has come under harsh criticism from supporters of the Efficient Markets Hypothesis.

Flavin, Kleidon, and Marsh as well as Merton[7] show that if you assume that firms pay dividends in such a way that a change in the dividend payment from quarter to quarter induces a corresponding change in all future expected dividends (for example, $1.00 or $2.00 forever after each boom or bust in Figure 1), simple violations of the variance limit should not be interpreted as obvious evidence against the Efficient Markets model. However, these papers still fail to explain the very dramatic violations of the bounds on rational volatility found by Shiller.[8]

FIGURE 1.4 Market Price and Perfect Forecast Price: Variable Discount Rates

Source: Shiller, Robert, *Market Volatility,* The MIT Press, Cambridge, MA, 1990, p. 82.

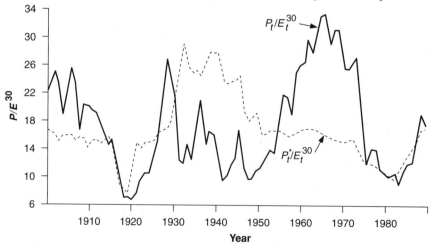

Moreover, Shiller's price volatility mystery is only the beginning. Stock prices aren't the only feature of stock market behavior that's too volatile.

As we shall see next, *volatility itself* is much too volatile!

THE SECOND MYSTERY:
STOCK *VOLATILITY* IS TOO UNSTABLE

Volatility in the Efficient Market

If stock pricing were fully rational, prices would move only in response to new and unanticipated information about prospects for firms and changing general economic conditions. The volatility of price changes would be based on the intensity of the flow of new information.

For *individual firms,* one might expect the intensity of the inflow of new information about firm prospects and economic conditions to vary considerably over time. For example, uncertainty is likely to increase just before earnings announcement dates, during labor disputes, litigation, takeovers, competitive bidding for important contracts, and the introduction of new products and advances into new markets.

For the *market aggregate,* however, the occurrence and timing of these events are likely to be well diversified over the individual firms in the index. This being the case, if the only source of market volatility was real news, you would expect the volatility of the stock market to be relatively stable over time.

Volatile Volatility

But market volatility is not stable. It is, itself, highly volatile.

I know this to be true because, a few years ago, I participated in a study of market reactions to shifts in the level of market volatility with two other professors, Eli Talmor and Walter Torous. (The three of us will hereafter be referred to as HTT.)

HTT focused on the daily fluctuations of the Dow Jones Industrial Average over the period 1897 through 1988. The idea for the study came after the turmoil of the October 19, 1987, crash. The crash was accompanied by a sudden and dramatic *sevenfold* increase[9] in the level of volatility. It occurred to HTT that some changes in volatility might come in *shifts* rather than as a process of gradual evolution. HTT also noted that similar bursts in volatility had occurred in the immediate vicinity of other similar market events like the 1929 crash.

Might there be a causal connection between the burst in the level of volatility and the simultaneous drop in the level of stock prices?

To answer this question, HTT designed a procedure to measure the reaction of stock prices to shifts in the level of volatility.[10]

All the volatility shifts found by their method are plotted as dots in Figure 1.5. Each of the dots in the top part of the diagram indicates a volatility increase. The scale to the right indicates the ratio of the variances (as you may recall, that's the square of volatility) after and before the shift. Volatility decreases are shown in the bottom part of the diagram. The time-series of volatility measured over a moving four-week period is plotted in the center of the graph. The scale for this time-series is shown to the left.

It is obvious that the volatility shifts are common events, occurring, on average, *five times per year.*

Is it even remotely possible that the uncertainty associated with underlying business conditions is shifting this often? Is it really possible that changes in economic uncertainty are responsible for the apparent instability in the market volatility series at the center of Figure 1.5?

Table 1.1 shows the number of events by decade as well as the magnitude of the volatilities in the leading and trailing blocks. Note that the sizes of the

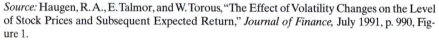

FIGURE 1.5 Market Volatility and Volatility Increase and Decrease Events

Source: Haugen, R. A., E. Talmor, and W. Torous, "The Effect of Volatility Changes on the Level of Stock Prices and Subsequent Expected Return," *Journal of Finance,* July 1991, p. 990, Figure 1.

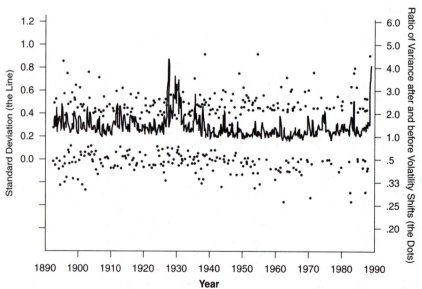

TABLE 1.1	Identified Volatility Shifts		
Time Period	*Number of Events*	*Average Prior Volatility*	*Average Subsequent Volatility*
A: Volatility Increases			
1897–1988	205	.102	.230
1897–1899	6	.125	.295
1900–1909	28	.101	.234
1910–1919	28	.108	.222
1920–1929	23	.110	.243
1930–1939	24	.183	.404
1940–1949	27	.074	.171
1950–1959	23	.064	.141
1960–1969	20	.063	.133
1970–1979	10	.093	.215
1980–1988	16	.105	.291
B: Volatility Decreases			
1897–1988	197	.231	.110
1897–1899	5	.263	.129
1900–1909	32	.235	.107
1910–1919	24	.226	.107
1920–1929	21	.208	.103
1930–1939	32	.374	.196
1940–1949	28	.161	.075
1950–1959	18	.143	.067
1960–1969	18	.143	.064
1970–1979	9	.207	.101
1980–1988	10	.337	.125

Source: Haugen, R. A., E. Talmor, and W. Torous, "The Effect of Volatility Changes on the Level of Stock Prices and Subsequent Expected Return," *Journal of Finance,* July 1991, p. 991, Table 1.

shifts are large; we are typically observing more than a doubling or a halving in volatility.

Reaction of Price Level to Volatility Shifts

Having identified the time-incidence of volatility shifts, HTT now examine the reaction of the *level* of stock prices to shifts in volatility.

Centering the two blocks at the point immediately before each shift detected, they measure the total percentage change in the level of the market index that occurs in the leading block. Presumably, as investors move into the event, they become aware that volatility has changed. The "rules of the game" have suddenly changed. In the case of a volatility increase, the probability of large price changes (up or down) occurring in a single day has increased. Investors may gain this awareness on the basis of the occurrence of some real event, such as the bombing of Pearl Harbor or, perhaps, simply by watching the day-to-day volatility of prices themselves.

In any case, they become aware that the risk associated with stock investments has changed. We know that most investors are risk-averse. If volatility has increased, they will want to earn a higher rate of return in the future on their stock investments. If nothing associated with the volatility shift has changed the prospects for future dividends, the only way future return will be higher is if the price you have to pay today for a stock is lower.

Thus, a volatility increase calls for a drop in the level of stock prices. And the bigger the increase in volatility and the longer the volatility increase is expected to "stick around," the larger the drop in stock prices should be.

The average percentage changes in the level of the market index in the four weeks preceding and following the beginning of a volatility increase is presented in Table 1.2a. The results are presented by decade, and the overall results are presented at the top of the table.

Overall, the price reaction to a volatility increase is negative.[11] Statistical analysis indicates a very low probability that the results are due to chance. This is confirmed by the fact that in all but one of the decades examined, the mean reaction is negative and statistically significant.[12]

Table 1.2b shows the corresponding results for volatility decreases. Here we see the opposite pattern, with the level of the index going up in nearly every decade, in response to a lowering of the required rate of return by investors.[13]

The time patterns of the price reactions to volatility increases and decreases, respectively, are shown in Figures 1.6a and 1.6b on pp. 13 and 14. The figures plot the average cumulative percentage changes in the value of the Dow from 20 days preceding the event to 30 days after it. Note that, for increases, the price decline dissipates after approximately 17 days. For decreases, the price advance continues for 21 days. There is also no evidence of a tendency of the market to correct its price adjustment.

Realization of the New Expected Returns

If prices are adjusting to provide higher (lower) returns to investors during a volatility increase (decrease), the higher (lower) expected returns should, on average, be realized during the period following the price adjustment.

TABLE 1.2a   Market Response to Volatility Increases

Time Period	Number of Events	Average 4-week Percentage Price Changes	
		Trailing Block (%)	*Leading Block (%)*
Total Period	205	1.269	−2.622
		.001	.000
1890s	6	3.604	−6.596
		.040	.020
1900s	28	2.007	−2.837
		.046	.016
1910s	28	2.416	−2.068
		.023	.062
1920s	23	3.132	−3.048
		.016	.037
1930s	24	−.558	−4.395
		.769	.052
1940s	27	.727	−2.847
		.101	.013
1950s	23	1.580	−2.188
		.015	.001
1960s	20	−.079	−2.825
		.917	.006
1970s	10	−2.811	−2.618
		.020	.042
1980s	16	1.863	1.549
		.047	.474

Note: This table shows average four-week percentage price changes surrounding volatility increases. These results are presented for the entire sample period, as well as by decades. Directly below the mean return I provide the probability that the mean return is zero.

Source: Haugen, R. A., E. Talmor, and W. Torous, "The Effect of Volatility Changes on the Level of Stock Prices and Subsequent Expected Return," *Journal of Finance,* July 1991, p. 995, Table III.

To see if this happens, HTT look at the percentage changes in price during a third block of time. The block also covers 4 weeks.[14]

Following the price adjustment (in the leading block) accompanying volatility increases, the average (across all increases in all years) annualized percentage change in price is 4.57%. Following decreases it is −.0014%.[15]

We can say with 97% confidence that price returns following increases are greater than those following decreases.

TABLE 1.2b Market Response to Volatility Decreases

Time Period	Number of Events	Average 4-week Percentage Price Changes Trailing Block (%)	Leading Block (%)
Total period	197	.472	1.703
		.248	.000
1890s	5	−.0899	3.157
		.803	.032
1900s	32	−.240	1.499
		.738	.018
1910s	24	−.100	1.762
		.925	.020
1920s	21	1.110	3.161
		.323	.000
1930s	32	1.401	1.672
		.377	.205
1940s	28	.413	1.345
		.632	.010
1950s	18	−1.138	2.832
		.184	.000
1960s	18	.765	1.860
		.397	.001
1970s	9	2.661	−1.284
		.148	.420
1980s	10	1.056	−.106
		.729	.927

Note: This table shows average 4-week percentage price changes surrounding volatility decreases. These results are presented for the entire sample period, as well as by decades. Directly below the mean return I provide the probability that the mean return is zero.

Source: Haugen, R. A., E. Talmor, and W. Torous, "The Effect of Volatility Changes on the Level of Stock Prices and Subsequent Expected Return, *Journal of Finance,* July 1991, p. 996, Table IV.

Investors evidently *require* a premium and they *are* being compensated for sailing through choppy waters. They are willing to accept a lower rate of compensation if the seas are tranquil.

The Crash Fits

If price adjustments following volatility shifts are, indeed, associated with changing required future returns, the magnitudes of the price adjustments in the leading block should be positively related to the size of the volatility shift. Interestingly, HTT find no significant link between price adjustment and the magnitude of volatility decreases. But they do find a strong relationship for volatility increases.

For increases, we can expect a downward price adjustment of 40 basis points for each multiple increase in the *variance.* Larger price adjustments can be ex-

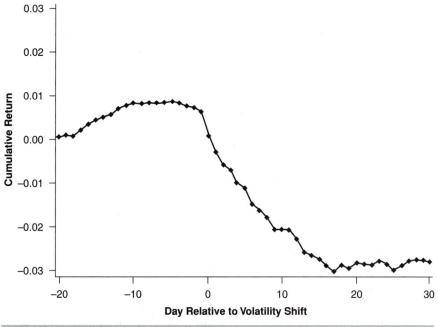

FIGURE 1.6a Cumulative Returns for Volatility Increases *(averaged over all increases)*

Source: Haugen, R. A., E. Talmor, and W. Torous, "The Effect of Volatility Changes on the Level of Stock Prices and Subsequent Expected Return," *Journal of Finance,* July 1991, p. 999, Figure 2.

pected to bring higher returns following the adjustment because investors require higher returns to sail through stronger storms.

And what about a hurricane?

In the four weeks starting October 19, 1987, the market's *variance* (volatility squared) increased by nearly 43 times over the four weeks prior to the crash.[16]

Based on HTT's measured relationship between the size of a volatility increase and the corresponding expected price response, we would have expected a price decline in the four weeks following the crash of over 17%.[17]

This is somewhat less than the drop actually experienced; however, much of the decline experienced on October 19 can be attributed to portfolio insurance, which exacerbated the market's reaction to the volatility increase.[18]

It would seem that the 1987 crash may have been related to a volatility shift.

The Events behind the Shifts

But what *caused* the shift?

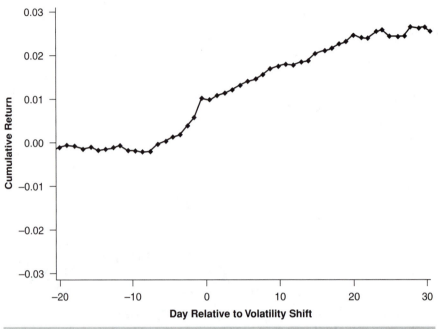

FIGURE 1.6b Cumulative Returns for Volatility Decreases *(averaged over all decreases)*

Source: Haugen, R. A., E. Talmor, and W. Torous, "The Effect of Volatility Changes on the Level of Stock Prices and Subsequent Expected Return," *Journal of Finance,* July 1991, p. 999, Figure 2.

Indeed, what types of events, in general, trigger the ups and downs we see in price volatility? HTT attempted to answer this question by looking for major events reported in the media around the time of their volatility events.[19]

Clearly, based on what was happening to volatility, something extraordinary was happening in the stock market. Was anything extraordinary happening *in the world* that the market may have been reacting to?

Interestingly, in approximately 9 out of 10 cases, *nothing of significance can be found in the reports of the media.* In many cases following volatility increases, the focus was on the market itself and its strange behavior.

In those few cases where HTT find that something interesting *was* happening in the real world, an interesting dichotomy emerges between the types of events that are typically associated with volatility increases versus the types that are associated with decreases.

Table 1.3a lists all the real world events found in the vicinity of those volatility increases that could be linked to a real event.

TABLE 1.3a   Extraordinary Events Associated with the Few Volatility Increases Where a Contributing Event Could Be Found

Volatility Shift Date	Event	Price Return in Second Block (%)	Variance Ratio
02/14/1898	Battleship Maine explodes in Havana, effectively beginning Spanish-American War	−10.47	4.12
08/13/1898	Spanish-American War ends	2.52	4.05
04/15/1901	Philippine rebellion ended by proclamation	−4.92	13.45
09/06/1901	President McKinley shot in Buffalo	−14.02	5.73
12/05/1904	Monroe Doctrine strengthened and reasserted by Roosevelt	−3.17	8.88
08/29/1905	Treaty of Portsmouth signed	−1.01	6.73
04/18/1906	Major earthquake in San Francisco	−3.68	4.60
10/09/1907	Bank panic	−13.61	3.15
06/16/1916	U.S. invades Mexico	−6.75	4.00
02/01/1917	President Wilson informs Congress he has broken diplomatic relations with Germany	−2.27	4.16
08/01/1927	President Coolidge announces that he will not run for reelection	3.75	6.24
09/17/1931	Bank panic	−14.90	11.93
02/09/1933	Federal banking holiday	−.36	12.15
07/16/1934	The first general strike in U.S. history	−8.86	4.89
08/18/1937	Miller-Tydings Enabling Act	−13.36	13.37
08/16/1939	Germany invades Poland	9.60	5.67
05/10/1940	Germany invades Holland and Belgium	−21.36	31.37
12/02/1941	Japan bombs Pearl Harbor	−1.77	4.63
06/05/1944	D-Day	4.32	3.83
11/01/1948	President Truman upsets Dewey	−7.99	6.98
10/19/1951	President Truman signs tax increase bill	−4.72	4.69
09/22/1955	President Eisenhower's heart attack	−6.42	33.05
08/06/1956	National steel strike ends	−3.46	3.34
10/30/1963	President Kennedy's assassination	−1.13	12.03
11/01/1971	President Nixon's economic policy	.08	15.57
04/15/1983	U.S. Embassy in Lebanon blown up	5.09	15.52
02/03/1984	Soviet President Andropov dies	−3.36	8.58
03/27/1987	President Reagan announces 100% tariffs on Japanese electronics	−5.55	5.13
	Averages	−4.56	9.21

Source: Haugen, R. A., E. Talmor, and W. Torous, "The Effect of Volatility Changes on the Level of Stock Prices and Subsequent Expected Return," *Journal of Finance,* July 1991, p. 993, Table IIA.

The common element linking nearly all the events is *violence*. By a government. By an individual. Or even by an act of nature.

Table 1.3b is for the few decreases that could be linked to a real world event. The common element here seems to be political enactments or proclamations of one sort or another.

Apparently, when the government takes action, the market calms down.

TABLE 1.3b Extraordinary Events Associated with the Few Volatility Decreases Where a Contributing Event Could Be Found

Volatility Shift Date	Event	Price Return in Leading Block (%)	Variance Ratio
03/02/1901	Pratt Amendment adopted	2.49	.18
01/20/1902	U.S. buys Virgin Islands from Denmark	2.80	.30
10/10/1902	Commission named to settle coal miners' strike	–1.27	.35
08/01/1905	Peace conference opens to end Russo-Japanese War	6.71	.20
01/11/1909	U.S. and Great Britain sign U.S.-Canada boundary waters treaty	–.82	.26
07/01/1909	Congress proposes the adoption of income tax	4.24	.34
01/14/1932	Congress creates the Reconstruction Finance Corporation	–14.45	.32
05/15/1933	Tennessee Valley Authority is established	20.12	.36
06/16/1934	Securities Exchange Commission created	.43	.22
03/11/1941	President Roosevelt signs Lend-Lease Act	.02	.18
07/30/1941	President Roosevelt and Prime Minister Churchill sign Atlantic Charter	–2.02	.32
11/18/1942	President Roosevelt orders nationwide gas rationing	2.22	.35
09/20/1945	Coal mines close as strikes break out	3.27	.29
11/07/1946	President Truman removes wage, price, and salary controls	.96	.24
01/17/1963	Strike of East and Gulf Coast longshoremen ends	1.92	.18
09/08/1971	President Nixon discloses his intentions for Phase II of his economic program	–2.74	.06
04/23/1980	Iranian hostage rescue mission fails	5.44	.23
04/15/1988	U.S. and Iran clash in Persian Gulf	–1.82	.22
	Averages	1.51	.26

Source: Haugen, R. A., E. Talmor, and W. Torous, "The Effect of Volatility Changes on the Level of Stock Prices and Subsequent Expected Return," *The Journal of Finance,* July 1991, p. 994, Table IIB.

Taking Stock

Before moving to the third mystery, we should take stock of what we have learned thus far:

- Stock prices are arguably too volatile, relative to the dividends and underlying cash flows that they are based upon.
- Stock volatility itself seems too unstable, shifting, on average, five times each year.
- The nature of price reactions accompanying volatility shifts seems consistent with adjustments to provide investors with higher (lower) returns to compensate them for staying in the market during choppy (tranquil) periods. This is confirmed by the significant differences between the realizations of return following the price adjustments associated with volatility increases and decreases.
- For volatility increases, the magnitude of the price adjustment tends to correspond to the magnitude of the volatility shift. The price reaction of October 1987 fits nicely with this pattern.
- No real economic, political, or other events of significance can be associated with the vast majority of volatility shifts.

THE THIRD MYSTERY:
NOISE IN THE MARKET—SILENCE ON THE STREET

Do Economic/Financial Conditions
Drive the Stock Market?

As we saw above, approximately 9 out of 10 shifts in volatility seem to be isolated events, occurring on their own, independent from any driver from the world outside the market.

Forget your inability to predict the *future* course of the market index. We shall see now that our ability to explain why the market has moved *in the past* is also shockingly low—at least when we attempt to explain market moves on the basis of changes in fundamental variables describing economic, business, and financial conditions.

The very large fraction of market volatility that goes unexplained has been alluded to by several of the leaders of academic finance,[20] but the important implications of this facet of the market's character have been largely, and conveniently, ignored.

In an interesting study, Cutler, Poterba, and Summers (CPS)[21] try to account for differences in the month-to-month rates of return to the market index[22] on the basis of unexpected changes[23] in the following economic and financial variables:

- Inflation-adjusted dividends paid to the index.
- Industrial production.
- Inflation-adjusted money supply.
- High-grade corporate bond yields.
- Treasury bill yields.
- Rate of inflation
- Daily stock price volatility within the month.

Over the period 1926 through 1986, CPS find that combined, unexpected changes in these important and closely watched economic and financial variables are able to explain only 18% of the differences in the monthly rates of return to the index. Fully 82% of the variability in return is attributable to unknown forces.

Increases in the first three variables have a positive effect on the market's return; the last four variables have a negative effect. However, only dividends, industrial production, and *volatility* have a statistically significant effect.

Note that volatility comes up significant again! If the market's volatility is high during a particular month, the return tends to be low.[24]

The low return may again be the result of the price adjustment required to provide investors with a higher future return during the period of high volatility in the following weeks or months.

Price Reactions to Historic Events

Surprised at the low power of these important economic variables at explaining market behavior, CPS now focus on the market's reaction to extraordinary, even historic, real world events that have taken place since 1941.[25]

The events are listed in Table 1.4a. The right-hand column lists the market's rate of return on each particular day.

The returns are large in absolute value, *but not that large*. The average absolute percentage change in the value of the index during these historic days is 1.46%.

To put this number in perspective, although it is approximately 2.6 times larger than the market's average percentage move across all days since 1941, the market's average absolute move in a single day is .56% with a standard deviation of .82%.

This means that for approximately one-third of the total number of days since 1941, the market's daily percentage change could be expected to exceed 1.38%

TABLE 1.4a   Major Events and Changes in the S&P Index, 1941–1987

Event	Date	% Change
Japanese bomb Pearl Harbor	Dec. 8, 1941	–4.37
U.S. declares war against Japan	Dec. 9, 1941	–3.23
Roosevelt defeats Dewey	Nov. 8, 1944	–0.15
Roosevelt dies	Apr. 13, 1945	1.07
Atomic bombs dropped on Japan:		
Hiroshima bomb	Aug. 6, 1945	0.27
Nagasaki bomb; Russia declares war	Aug. 9, 1945	1.65
Japanese surrender	Aug. 17, 1945	–0.54
Truman defeats Dewey	Nov. 3, 1948	–4.61
North Korea invades South Korea	June 26, 1950	–5.38
Truman to send U.S. troops	June 27, 1950	–1.10
Eisenhower defeats Stevenson	Nov. 5, 1952	0.28
Eisenhower suffers heart attack	Sept. 26, 1955	–6.62
Eisenhower defeats Stevenson	Nov. 7, 1956	–1.03
U-2 shot down; U.S. admits spying	May 9, 1960	0.09
Kennedy defeats Nixon	Nov. 9, 1960	0.44
Bay of Pigs invasion announced;	Apr. 17, 1961	0.47
Details released over several days	Apr. 18, 1961	–0.72
	Apr. 19, 1961	–0.59
Cuban missile crisis begins:		
Kennedy announces Russian buildup	Oct. 23, 1962	–2.67
Soviet letter stresses peace	Oct. 24, 1962	3.22
Formula to end dispute reached	Oct. 29, 1962	2.16
Kennedy assassinated;	Nov. 22, 1963	–2.81
Orderly transfer of power to Johnson	Nov. 26, 1963	3.98
U.S. fires on Vietnamese ship	Aug. 4, 1964	–1.25
Johnson defeats Goldwater	Nov. 4, 1964	–0.05
Johnson withdraws from race, halts Vietnamese raids, urges peace talks	Apr. 1, 1968	2.53
Robert Kennedy assassinated	June 5, 1968	–0.49
Nixon defeats Humphrey	Nov. 6, 1968	0.16
Nixon imposes price controls, requests Federal tax cut, strengthens dollar	Aug. 16, 1971	3.21
Nixon defeats McGovern	Nov. 8, 1972	0.55
Haldeman, Ehrlichman, and Dean resign	Apr. 30, 1973	–0.24
Dean tells Senate about Nixon cover-up	June 25, 1973	–1.40
Agnew resigns	Oct. 10, 1973	–0.83
Carter defeats Ford	Nov. 3, 1976	–1.14
Volcker appointed to Fed	July 25, 1979	1.09
Fed announces major policy changes	Oct. 6, 1979	–1.25
Soviet Union invades Afghanistan	Dec. 26, 1979	0.11
Attempt to free Iranian hostages fails	Apr. 26, 1980	0.73

TABLE 1.4a *(cont.)*		
Event	*Date*	*%* *Change*
Reagan defeats Carter	Nov. 5, 1980	1.77
Reagan shot, NYSE closes early;	Mar. 30, 1981	−0.27
Reopens next day	Mar. 31, 1981	1.28
U.S. Marines killed in Lebanon	Oct. 24, 1983	0.02
U.S. invades Grenada	Oct. 25, 1983	0.29
Reagan defeats Mondale	Nov. 7, 1984	1.09
House votes for Tax Reform Act of 1986	Dec. 18, 1985	−0.40
Chernobyl nuclear reactor meltdown;	Apr. 29, 1986	−1.06
Details released over several days	Apr. 30, 1986	−2.07
Senate Committee votes for tax reform	May 8, 1986	−0.49
Greenspan named to replace Volcker	June 2, 1987	−0.47
Important Events		
Average Absolute Return		1.46
Standard Deviation of Returns		2.08
All Days since 1941		
Average Absolute Return		0.56
Standard Deviation of Returns		0.82

(.56% + .82%) in absolute value.[26] (For a bell curve, one standard deviation above and below the mean includes two-thirds of the expected observations.)

In this context, a 1.46% rate of return doesn't seem extraordinary at all.

Ordinary market reactions to truly extraordinary real world events.

The Events Associated with Big Price Reactions

If the market isn't reacting to (a) changes in important economic variables and (b) historic events, just what *is* it reacting to?

To help find an answer to this question, CPS now examines the events behind the market's largest single-day moves.

In Table 1.4b they list, in order of absolute magnitude, the 50 largest 1-day percentage changes in the S&P Index. Listed, along with the percentage changes, is the *New York Times* account of the fundamental factors responsible for the change.

These are some of the most extraordinary events in the history of the stock market.

Yet, for the most part, they don't seem to be connected to extraordinary events happening in the real world!

	Date	% Change	New York Times *Explanation*[a]
			TABLE 1.4b Fifty Largest Postwar Movements in S&P Index and Their "Causes"
1	Oct. 19, 1987	−20.47	Worry over dollar decline and trade deficit, fear of U.S. not supporting dollar.
2	Oct. 21, 1987	9.10	Interest rates continue to fall; deficit talks in Washington; bargain hunting.
3	Oct. 26, 1987	−8.28	Fear of budget deficits; margin calls; reaction to falling foreign stocks.
4	Sept. 3, 1946	−6.73	"No basic reason for the assault on prices."
5	May 28, 1962	−6.68	Kennedy forces rollback of steel price hike.
6	Sept. 26, 1955	−6.62	Eisenhower suffers heart attack.
7	June 26, 1950	−5.38	Outbreak of Korean War.
8	Oct. 20, 1987	5.33	Investors looking for "quality stocks."
9	Sept. 9, 1946	−5.24	Labor unrest in maritime and trucking industries.
10	Oct. 16, 1987	−5.16	Fear of trade deficit; fear of higher interest rates; tension with Iran.
11	May 27, 1970	5.02	Rumors of change in economic policy. "The stock surge happened for no fundamental reason."
12	Sept. 11, 1986	−4.81	Foreign governments refuse to lower interest rates; crackdown on triple witching announced.
13	Aug. 17, 1982	4.76	Interest rates decline.
14	May 29, 1962	4.65	Optimistic brokerage letters; institutional and corporate buying; suggestions of tax cut.
15	Nov. 3, 1948	−4.61	Truman defeats Dewey.
16	Oct. 9, 1974	4.60	Ford to reduce inflation and interest rates.
17	Feb. 25, 1946	−4.57	Weakness in economic indicators over past week.
18	Oct. 23, 1957	4.49	Eisenhower urges confidence in economy.
19	Oct. 29, 1987	4.46	Deficit reduction talks begin; durable goods orders increase; rallies overseas.
20	Nov. 5, 1948	−4.40	Further reaction to Truman victory over Dewey.
21	Nov. 6, 1946	−4.31	Profit taking; Republican victories in elections presage deflation.
22	Oct. 7, 1974	4.19	Hopes that President Ford would announce strong anti-inflationary measures.
23	Nov. 30, 1987	−4.18	Fear of dollar fall.
24	July 12, 1974	4.08	Reduction in new loan demands; lower inflation previous month.
25	Oct. 15, 1946	4.01	Meat prices decontrolled; prospects of other decontrols.
26	Oct. 25, 1982	−4.00	Disappointment over Federal Reserve's failure to cut discount rates.
27	Nov. 26, 1963	3.98	Confidence in Johnson after Kennedy assassination.
28	Nov. 1, 1978	3.97	Steps by Carter to strengthen dollar.
29	Oct. 22, 1987	−3.92	Iranian attack on Kuwaiti oil terminal; fall in markets overseas; analysts predict lower prices.

TABLE 1.4b *(cont.)*

	Date	% Change	New York Times *Explanation*[a]
30	Oct. 29, 1974	3.91	Decline in short-term interest rates; ease in future monetary policy; lower oil prices.
31	Nov. 3, 1982	3.91	Relief over small Democratic victories in House.
32	Feb. 19, 1946	−3.70	Fear of wage-price controls lowering corporate profits; labor unrest.
33	June 19, 1950	−3.70	Korean War continues; fear of long war.
34	Nov. 18, 1974	−3.67	Increase in unemployment rate; delay in coal contract approval; fear of new Middle-East war.
35	Apr. 22, 1980	3.64	Fall in short-term interest rates; analysts express optimism.
36	Oct. 31, 1946	3.63	Increase in commodity prices; prospects for price decontrol.
37	July 6, 1955	3.57	Market optimism triggered by GM stock split.
38	June 4, 1962	−3.55	Profit taking; continuation of previous week's decline.
39	Aug. 20, 1982	3.54	Congress passes Reagan tax bill; prime rate falls.
40	Dec. 3, 1987	−3.53	Computerized selling; November retail sales low.
41	Sept. 19, 1974	3.50	Treasury Secretary Simon predicts decline in short-term interest rates.
42	Dec. 9, 1946	3.44	Coal strike ends; railroad freight rates increase.
43	June 29, 1962	3.44	"Stock prices advanced strongly chiefly because they had gone down so long and so far that a rally was due."
44	Sept. 5, 1946	3.43	"Replacement buying" after earlier fall.
45	Oct. 30, 1987	3.33	Dollar stabilizes; increase in prices abroad.
46	Jan. 27, 1975	3.27	IBM wins appeal of antitrust case; short-term interest rates decline.
47	Oct. 6, 1982	3.27	Interest rates fall; several large companies announce increase in profits.
48	July 19, 1948	−3.26	Worry over Russian blockade of Berlin; possibility of more price controls.
49	Nov. 30, 1982	3.22	"Analysts were at a loss to explain why the Dow jumped so dramatically in the last two hours."
50	Oct. 24, 1962	3.22	Krushchev promises no rash decisions on Cuban missile crisis; calls for U.S.-Soviet summit.

[a]Per the financial section or front page.

Source: Cutler, David, James Poterba and Lawrence Summers, "What Moves Stock Price?" *Journal of Portfolio Management,* Spring 1989, pp. 144–147, Tables 3 and 4.

The Events Associated with the Big Bursts in Volatility

In their paper, Haugen, Talmor, and Torous do a similar analysis for the largest volatility shifts.

Table 1.5 lists the 20 largest volatility increases in the period 1897 through 1988. Once again, as discussed earlier, HTT search the media for real-world events that might be responsible for the extreme chaos occurring in the market.

As indicated in Table 1.5, for most of these truly historic *financial* events, the market seems to be acting of its own accord, with no stimulus from the outside.

For most of these events, the market doesn't seem to be reacting to an external signal coming from the real world.

Is it possible that the signal is coming from within the market itself?[27]

What is this fundamental driver behind the market's behavior?

Orange Juice

Interestingly, the stock market isn't the only speculative market for which it is difficult to explain fluctuations in prices on the basis of fluctuations in those fundamental factors that, rationally, should play a dominant role in price determination.

TABLE 1.5	News Released in Vicinity of Largest Volatility Increases[a]	
Event Period	*Increase in Volatility (%)*	*Release of Extraordinary Economic Information*
12/04/1899–01/02/1900	402	None
04/15/1901–05/14/1901	267	None
05/18/1903–06/15/1903	213	None
03/04/1907–04/01/1907	305	None
01/13/1910–02/09/1910	250	None
10/05/1929–11/06/1929	300	None
09/17/1931–10/15/1931	245	Bank panic
02/09/1933–03/21/1933	249	Federal banking holiday
08/18/1937–09/15/1937	266	None
05/10/1940–06/08/1940	460	Germany invades Holland and Belgium
07/26/1943–08/21/1943	221	None
06/28/1945–07/31/1945	238	None
08/27/1946–09/30/1946	239	None
06/05/1950–07/07/1950	329	Korean war begins
09/22/1955–10/19/1955	475	President Eisenhower's heart attack
10/30/1963–11/29/1963	247	President Kennedy's assassination
07/27/1971–08/23/1971	295	President Nixon's economic policy
04/15/1983–05/12/1983	294	None
06/27/1983–07/25/1983	331	None
10/06/1987–11/02/1987	478	None

[a]In this table, volatility is measured by standard deviation of returns.

Source: Haugen, R. A., E. Talmor, and W. Torous, "The Effect of Volatility Changes on the Level of Stock Prices and Subsequent Expected Return," *Journal of Finance,* July 1991, p. 1003, Table VII.

Take the commodity market, for example.

Orange Juice.

What should be the driver behind the price of frozen orange juice futures contracts?

The price of orange juice should be determined by the intersection of supply and demand, as in Figure 1.7. I have drawn the figure on the assumption that the demand for orange juice is somewhat sensitive to its price. If there is a significant increase in the price of orange juice, some of us will want to switch to grapefruit or pineapple. This represents movement up and down the demand curve.

Shifts in the demand curve mean that people would want to buy more or less orange juice *at a given price*. What would cause that in the short-term?

A change in our tastes.[28] Suddenly, significant numbers of us want to drink more or less of it. But this isn't likely to happen. In the short-term, the demand curve for orange juice is likely to be relatively stable.

What about the supply curve?

Producers can supply more orange juice by planting more trees. But this isn't likely to affect the supply of the juice in the near-term. Orange trees take from 5 to 10 years to reach maturity.

What will change supply in the near-term?

Weather.

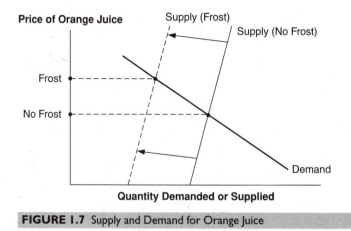

FIGURE 1.7 Supply and Demand for Orange Juice

The combination of temperature and precipitation can produce a vintage year or a disaster over a growing season. Weather can move the supply curve causing growers to supply more or less at a given price. For example, a major frost in Florida can result in a backward shift in the supply curve to the broken line, resulting in an increase in the price of orange juice.

Weather should be the *major* determinant of the price of orange juice.

Does Weather Drive the Price of Orange Juice?

To see if this was true, Richard Roll studied the determinants of the prices of orange juice futures contracts.[29]

Noting that more than 98% of U.S. production is concentrated in the central Florida region around Orlando, he concentrates on the effect of weather in this location on the price.

Roll finds that percentage changes in orange juice futures are significantly related to temperature, especially cold temperatures, in the Orlando area. He even finds a statistically significant relation between percentage changes in the price of orange juice futures and *subsequent* errors in the forecasts of temperature made by the National Weather Service.

Roll finds that the futures market actually seems to be out-forecasting the national weather service. However, Roll finds no relationship between changes in orange juice futures prices and unexpected rainfall.

He also looks at energy related factors (which could affect the costs of distribution and operating farm equipment), the return to the stock market index, the Canadian dollar exchange rate (which may affect the demand for U.S. orange juice on the part of the largest foreign consumer), news stories that are related to orange juice in various ways, as well as the prices for substitute products.

He finds a real puzzle. He can explain less than 10% of the percentage changes in the futures price on the basis of *all* these factors.

But what accounts for the remaining 90% of the price fluctuations?

Because Roll seems to have exhausted the potentially important external drivers to the futures price of orange juice, the major driver may, once again, be internal to the futures market itself.

But what *is* this driver of stock and futures prices?

THE FOURTH MYSTERY:
THE SILENCE AFTER THE CLOSING BELL

Prices Still Move After the Market Is Closed

Security *values* change even when the securities themselves are not traded.

Those who have participated in the Southern California housing market know this all too well. Most are well aware of the fact that the market value of their individual homes has moved up and down like a roller coaster, although many haven't called the moving van out even once.

Trading isn't a *requirement* for price volatility. After the exchange closes, *things still happen.* In the economy. In politics. In foreign affairs. In other markets.

Even after the closing bell, the prices of stocks should still be responding to events as they happen. And the difference between today's closing price and tomorrow's opening price should collectively reflect these responses.

If stock market pricing is efficient and rational, the difference between the market's volatility when it is closed and when it is open should reflect the rate at which investors receive fresh information about their investments.

Measuring Volatility
When the Market Is Closed

If we can't see the prices move, how can we tell how volatile stock prices are when the market is closed?

Fortunately, the hour-to-hour changes in stock prices are pretty random.[30] This feature, as it turns out, provides us with a fairly good indicator of the action going on when the market is shut down.

If stock prices change randomly, the variance of return is proportional to the length of time over which the return is measured. For a given stock, or for the market index, the variance of 2-day returns should be twice as large as the variance of 1-day returns. Likewise, the variance of annual returns should be 12 times as large as the variance of monthly returns.

Orange Juice on Weekends

Just how volatile are prices on weekends when the exchange is closed?

Three days span the period from Saturday through Monday. If the volatility is the same on Saturday and Sunday as it is on a weekday, the variance of returns from the close on Friday through the close on Monday should be three times as great as the variance of return from the close on Thursday through the close on Friday.

Think about orange juice. As we discussed in the previous section, the major determinate of the price of orange juice futures is weather. Mother Nature doesn't know weekends from weekdays. The weather and forecasts of the weather go on unabated. This being the case, there should be nearly as much information being generated about orange juice on the weekend as on any other day.

In looking at close-to-close percentage changes in orange juice futures prices, Roll noticed that the variance of the percentage change from Fridays through Mondays was only 54% greater than the variance on the other weekdays.

If the variance on Saturday and Sunday were the same as on weekdays, it would have been 300% greater than the variance on weekdays. The fact that it was only 54% greater means that, on average, the variance on Saturday and on Sunday is only 27% as great as the variance on the other days.

Mother Nature doesn't rest on weekends.

And for weather-dominated orange juice, the major difference between Saturday and Sunday and the other days is the fact that juice futures aren't being traded on the futures exchange!

Common Stock on Weekends

This result apparently intrigued Roll. A short time later, he conducted a similar study with Ken French on the volatility of stock returns during different days of the week.[31]

They looked at daily close-to-close returns for individual stocks on the New York and American exchanges over the period 1963 through 1982.

Averaging over stocks and time, they found that the variance of Saturday through Monday's return was only 11% greater than the variance on other days. Again, this would imply that the variance on Saturday and Sunday was only 5.5% of the variance on the other days.

But it got *much* worse than that!

French and Roll (FR) calculated the difference in the variance in the *hours* when the exchange was open and when it was not.

During the time period FR studied, in the Saturday through Monday span, there were 66 closed hours and 6 open hours. On each of the other weekdays, there were 18 closed hours and 6 open hours.

FR found that the ratio of the variance over the total time (closed and open) on Saturday through Monday to the variance over the total time on the other days was 1.11.

We can now solve for the ratio of the market's variance when it is open to the variance when it is closed.[32] It is approximately 70.

What???

The variance of stock returns is 70 times greater when the exchange is open than when it is closed!

Volatility on Election Days and Exchange Holidays

Can it be that the flow of information coming in from the real world is this much more intense when the exchange is open?

FR also looks at the market's variance over holidays. On one-day holidays, the variance (over the total 24-hour period) is 11% of the 24-hour periods spanned by days when the exchange is open. For 2-day holidays, each of the two days has about 12% of the variance.

We know, however, at least in the far less global U.S. economic environment spanned by FR's study, that the flow of economic information is highly likely to slow down at night and on weekends and holidays. On average, in the hours when the market is closed, there will be a reduced flow of new information feeding into the reacting stock market.

But *70 times* more variance in the open hours?

To see if the difference in variances is related to differences in the flow of information, FR focused on election holidays and exchange holidays.

In their study period, there were many election days during which the stock exchanges were closed. One would expect that, on these days, the intensity of the flow of new information would be similar to (or greater than, in the case of political information) the flow on other days.

And what is an exchange holiday?

In 1968, the New York Stock Exchange was experiencing a backlog in its paperwork. A decision was made to close the Exchange on Wednesdays during the second half of the year in order to catch up.

On the exchange holidays, *everything* was running as usual *except for the New York Stock Exchange.*

So if we see a dramatic decline in stock price volatility during exchange holidays, this should tell us something very important: The major driving force behind the volatility of NYSE stocks is truly coming *from within the exchange itself!*

FR's evidence is presented in Table 1.6.

The table shows the average variance of return across the exchange and election holidays as a percent of the variance on other days. The results are shown for all stocks as well as for groups of different sizes in which the stocks are grouped on the basis of total market capitalization and split into equally weighted 20% size groupings.

On exchange holidays, for all stocks, the variance is only 14.5% of its value on other weekdays.[33] For election holidays, it is 16.5% of its value on other weekdays.

Note also that the variance ratio is larger for the larger stocks.

TABLE 1.6	Daily Variance Ratios for Exchange and Election Holidays (Ratios of Two-Day Holiday Variance to Single-Day Variance)					
		Daily Variance Ratios				
		All Stocks	*Smallest Quintile*[a]	*2*	*3*	*4*	*Largest Quintile*
Exchange holidays in 1968	Average ratio[b]	1.145	1.077	1.043	1.180	1.239	1.274
	Number of firms	2083	597	455	374	342	315
Election holidays	Average ratio[c]	1.165	1.131	1.073	1.186	1.159	1.332
	Number of firms	2026	572	426	367	347	314

[a]Firms are sorted into quintiles based on their relative total market capitalization.
[b]Average variance ratio comparing two-day exchange holiday returns with single-calendar-day returns.
[c]Average variance ratio comparing two-day election holiday returns with single-calendar-day returns.

Source: French, K. and R. Roll, "Stock Return Variances: The Arrival of Information and the Reaction of Traders," *Journal of Financial Economics,* 1986, pp. 5–26.

We can apply the same type of analysis used above to obtain an estimate of the ratio of the hourly variance when the exchange is open to the variance when it is closed.[34]

The market's variance, when it is open, is 25 times its variance when it is closed. This is less than the 70-fold difference found for weekends, but the generation of new information is likely to be much less on weekends than it is on exchange holidays.[35]

THE BEAST

We should also take note of the big differences between the estimates for small and large firms.

For the largest 20%, the variance is 12 times larger when the exchange is open.

For the smallest 20% the variance is nearly 50 times larger.

Whatever is causing the difference in volatility has a bigger impact on small firms than on large ones.[36] We should remember this when we look for its impact on other features of the market.[37]

We shall call this driver THE BEAST.

And we know now that it lives in the stock exchange.

The Pathetic Private Information Hypothesis

But French and Roll don't much believe in beasts. They think there's another reason for their finding that the market's variance is anywhere from 13 to 100 times larger when the exchange is open then when it is closed.

They believe that investors have more incentive to gather private information when the market is open than when it is closed.

You see, when the market is open, you can act on the gem of information that you find under the "stone" immediately. You don't have to wait until tomorrow when the stock exchange opens.

After all, if you wait until then, someone else may have found it. You may be waiting in line to buy or sell with a whole flock full of other investors ready to act on *their* gems. So you spend *much* more time (13 to 100 times more variance) looking for gems when the market is open.

Because of this, investors feel that *much* more information is revealed when the market is open than when it is closed.

This hypothesis is called the *Private Information Hypothesis*. It goes something like this . . .

The surface temperature of the Cross leather pad on Sandra Preston's antique cherry desk cooled yet another degree after baking most of the morning under the sun rising above Lake Michigan.

She had a great view of the lake across Michigan Avenue. Her father's investment advisory firm occupied the tenth and eleventh floors of the prestigious Hampton Towers, and she had the corner office on the tenth floor.

She was in charge. And she was ready. *Armed with an MBA from the University of Chicago! Her professors from Chicago knew how the markets worked and they had taught her very well.*

Yes. She was ready.

Through the northern glass wall of her office she watched Jim Foley talking on the phone to one of the telecommunications companies he followed. To his left was Jane Carrey. She was screening firms to find those that matched the firm's value requirements.

Preston and Grier was a value investment management firm. They looked for firms that were in reasonably sound financial condition, but selling at even less than reasonable prices.

Over on the western side of the office, the investment committee was debating the relative merits of the current list of candidate value stocks, trying to come up with this week's buys and sells for their composite portfolio.

Sandra looked at the matching cherry clock on her desk. 3:00 P.M. The market was now closed in New York. Time to put into action some of the things she learned at the university.

Her University of Chicago professors had taught her well about the relative value of information when the market is closed.

This firm could use an increase in efficiency!

She walked out of her office and confronted Foley. "Jim, please hang up the phone now.*"*

Foley looked confused. "Sandra, I'm talking to the CEO of Allied Communications. I've been trying to connect with this guy for weeks. What's the problem?"

"The problem is the market's closed. *Think about that. If he tells you something valuable* now, *you won't be able to act on it until* tomorrow. *Now hang up the phone and tell him you'll call back tomorrow at 8:30 A.M."*

"What the hell are you talking about? Do you think I can talk to this guy whenever I want? You must be joking. Right?"

"Sure Jim. I'm joking!*" Now hang up the phone!*

Sandra didn't care at all for his defiance of her authority. She walked over to his desk, took the receiver and promptly hung it up for him.

"The market is closed, and when the market is closed, we stop gathering information at Preston and Grier, because we want to be efficient!*"*

Now she marched to the desk of Jane Carrey. "Please turn off your computer, now!*"*

Carrey was actually startled. "But I've got to get the new value stock population to the investment committee by 4:00. I was late last week. If I'm late again, it could cost me my job!"

Sandra smiled. "Don't worry. I'm the one who determines that now. *Turn off your computer. The market is closed."*

"What do you mean the market is closed? What does that have to do with me?"

Sandra knew that she was going to have to deal with naiveté. If only everyone *was trained at Chicago. "Listen to me. The market is closed. What if you find something useful? Don't you see you won't be able to act on it until tomorrow? By then someone else may have found out about it. To be efficient, you shouldn't search for information until the market is* open. *That way you can act as soon as you find out about it."*

Carrey seemed perplexed. "Act? Do you mean trade? *I don't trade. I just report to the investment committee. Anything I find doesn't get acted upon for at least a week. They always want confirmation and* more confirmation.*"*

"We'll see about that."

Sandra Preston walked to the west conference room where the investment committee was in heated debate. She opened the door and walked in.

"This discussion must stop immediately."

Her father, Jeffery Preston, chairman of the committee, immediately stopped talking. "Sandra, what's the problem?"

"The market is closed."

"So what?"

"What do you mean, 'So what?' If you people come to any decision here this afternoon, you will have to wait until 8:30 tomorrow morning to act on it. You should talk tomorrow. You're wasting your time *talking now."*

Frank Grier, the firm's Chief Investment Officer broke in, "Wait a minute. We're trying to determine the week's buys and sells to be executed tomorrow at the opening bell. If we don't come to a decision now, we can't act tomorrow morning."

Sandra smiled. "The investment business is highly competitive. You know that. Much of this business is a process of discovery. When you discover things you must act quickly. *You must act before your competitors do. How can you act when the market is closed? See? To be efficient, you should only look for information when the market is open. This makes all the sense in the world to me. Why doesn't it make sense to all of you as well?"*

Grier: "What makes sense to me is that, if we stop searching for information when the market is closed, our competitors will find it before we do. I want my people looking 16 *hours a day. I want to find it first, damn it! Who cares if we have to wait for the bell to trade?"*

Jeffery Preston interjected, "Wait a minute, Frank. We can't be stuck in the past! We've got to be open to new ideas. Sandra's full of interesting new ideas from the University of Chicago. I think we should give them a chance."

Jeff Preston rose from his chair, and walked out of the conference room. He cupped his hands to his mouth and yelled.

"Everyone! Stop whatever you are doing and leave immediately! The market is closed. *I don't want to see anyone around here until 8:30 A.M. tomorrow. From now on we're running a 6½-hour day!"*

THE FIFTH MYSTERY: GOING GLOBAL EXTENDS THE LENGTH OF YOUR TRADING DAY AND THE RISK OF YOUR STOCK

Cross-Listed Stocks

If volatility goes down when the number of trading hours in a week decreases, the converse ought to be true as well. Volatility should become *greater* as the number of hours is *extended.*

But how to find a case of an increase in trading hours?

What about stocks that become cross-listed on the London Stock Exchanges? For these stocks, when the closing bell rings in New York, trading continues in London.

Several years ago, two University of Pittsburgh professors named Makhija and Nachtmann (MN) wrote a very interesting paper on the effects of cross-listing on stock volatility.[38] The paper was written when it was still gauche for financial economists to present evidence *against* the Efficient Market Hypothesis. This, in my view, is the likely reason this solid study, like many other papers providing evidence conflicting with the basic doctrines of Modern Finance, never saw the light of day and joined the others filling academic filing cabinets throughout the world.

If you would like a second opinion, Ken French (of FR) formally discussed the paper following its presentation by Makhija at the 1990 meetings of the Western Finance Association. Although expressing some chagrin over the nature of the findings, he could find little reason to fault the methodology.

Because the paper was never published, and is therefore largely unavailable to you, I'm going to spell out much of its detail in the footnotes.

Volatility and Cross-Listing

Makhija and Nachtmann studied 81 multinational firms, which were cross-listed on the London Stock Exchange over the period 1969 through 1982.[39]

As shown in Table 1.7a, the firms ranged in size from $40 million to $48 billion in total market capitalization (number of shares outstanding times market price per share). The average size was $2.15 billion and the median was $782 million. On average, a cross-listed firm represented 0.25 percent of the total market value of all firms on the New York and American stock exchanges.[40]

Considering the typical size of companies during the period of their study, these were, for the most part, large and well-established companies.

TABLE 1.7a Statistics for Cross-Listed Stocks, 1969–1982: Descriptive Statistics		
	Stock Value[a]	
	$	**% of Market**
Mean average	$2.149 billion	.248
Maximum	$48.360 billion	4.449
Minimum	$.040 billion	.004
Median	$.782 billion	.093

[a]Stock value is computed for individual firms as the product of shares outstanding and the closing price on date admitted to the LSE. Percent of market is computed for each stock as the ratio of the market value of the company's stock to the value of all stocks on the New York and American Stock Exchanges date of admission to the LSE.

Source: Adapted from Makhijan, A., and R. Nachtmann, 1989, "Empirical Evidence on Alternative Theories of Stock Return Variances: The Effect of Expanded Trading Time on NYSE–LSE Cross-Listed Stocks," unpublished manuscript, University of Pittsburgh.

Makhija and Nachtmann compute the variances of the daily rates of return to the stocks over the following time line:[41]

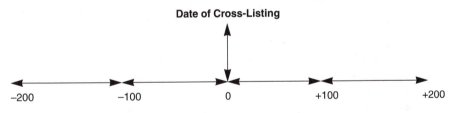

Date of Cross-Listing

−200   −100   0   +100   +200

Trading Days Relative to Cross-Listing Date

The first panel of Table 1.7b shows the average and median variances for the stocks in the periods ranging over 100 days prior to the cross-listing and from the cross-listing date to 100 days after. Note the rather dramatic increases in the variances of return.[42] In the second panel, the average and median variances are shown for the periods (−200 to −101) and (+101 to +200).

Again, note the substantial increases. Interestingly, variance continues to increase over the periods (0 to +100) and (+101 to +200).

Are these changes statistically significant? The first panel of Table 1.8 shows the average and median changes in the stocks computed over periods of 50, 100, and 200 days surrounding the cross-listing date. Statistical analysis indicates that the probability that cross-listing tends to be followed by a variance increase is astronomically high. The same is true for the medians.[43] Note also

TABLE 1.7b Statistics for Cross-Listed Stocks, 1969–1982: Daily Variance Estimates (in Basis Points) for Selected Intervals[a]

	Interior Intervals		Exterior Intervals	
	-100, -1	*+1, +100*	*-200, -101*	*+101, +200*
Mean average	3.55	4.53	3.57	5.31
Maximum	11.97	14.98	14.43	19.35
Minimum	.81	.68	.81	.74
Median	2.95	3.53	2.66	3.94

[a]Reported statistics on daily variance measures are computed for the interior times indicated using daily close-to-close NYSE rates of return.

Source: Adapted from Makhijan, A., and R. Nachtmann, 1989, "Empirical Evidence on Alternative Theories of Stock Return Variances: The Effect of Expanded Trading Time on NYSE–LSE Cross-Listed Stocks," unpublished manuscript, University of Pittsburgh.

TABLE 1.8 Volatility around Cross-Listing Dates for 81 Cross-Listed Stocks, 1969–1982

CHANGES IN FIRM VARIANCE

No. of Days Used to Compute Variance	% Change in Variance			% Change in Variance Relative to Market		
	200	*100*	*50*	*200*	*100*	*50*
Mean average	57[a]	35.77[a]	33.82[a]	32.14[a]	20.26[a]	21.81[b]
No. positive	60	57	52	53	52	45
No. negative	21	24	29	28	29	36
Median	39.05	20.15	8.54	15.48	13.18	8.97

[a]Significant with 99% confidence.
[b]Significant with 95% confidence.

Source: Adapted from Makhijan, A., and R. Nachtmann, 1989, "Empirical Evidence on Alternative Theories of Stock Return Variances: The Effect of Expanded Trading Time on NYSE–LSE Cross-Listed Stocks," unpublished manuscript, University of Pittsburgh.

that there are many more individual cases of variance increases following cross-listing than variance decreases.

Perhaps the trend in the level of volatility was upward during their study. Can we somehow abstract from movements in the general level of volatility and focus specifically on the effect of cross-listing?

The second panel of Table 1.8 shows the increases in the variances net of any increases in the variance experienced by the individual stocks comprising the market index.[44] Again the probabilities that cross-listing is associated with a *net* variance increase is extremely high.[45]

The Return of the Preposterous
Private Information Hypothesis

Makhija and Nachtmann admit that these results might be explained away by
advocates of the efficient markets on the basis of the so-called "private information hypothesis," which we discussed under the Fourth Mystery.

You see, public information includes items like earnings announcements
and court decisions. As soon as it is announced, such information affects prices
and causes volatility. Private information, on the other hand, is a product of the
analysis of "informed traders." Private information doesn't affect prices until
informed traders act on it and trade.

So how are Makhija and Nachtmann's results to be explained away by the
efficient markets types? Before cross-listing, informed traders had to wait until
the following morning to act on the private information their analysis produced
after the NYSE had closed. Since cross-listing on the LSE began, they can get in
there at 4:30 A.M. EST and trade like crazy! Because of the great new opportunity offered by cross-listing, those who believe in the private information hypothesis believe that informed traders will have an incentive to produce more
"private information" for cross-listed stocks, thereby driving up their volatility!

Somehow, this seems pretty far-fetched to me.[46] But when you attack the
Efficient Markets Hypothesis, you've got to be prepared for counterattacks by
the "Efficient Markets Police" from *every* possible direction.

Cross-Listing Makes the Market More Overreactive

To fend off the "private information" interpretation of their results, Makhija
and Nachtmann extend their study to an analysis of variance ratios.

As I previously discussed under the Fourth Mystery, if successive percentage
changes in stock prices are truly random and unconnected, volatility increases
proportionately with the time interval over which the percentage changes are
measured. The variance of annual returns will be 12 times as large as the variance
of monthly returns.

However, if stock markets are populated by traders who overreact to in-
coming information, successive changes in stock prices will *not* be random.

Suppose a positive piece of information comes into the market. Prices go
up, but by too much. This overreaction is then corrected by a fall in prices.

If traders are overreactive, we should see reversal patterns in stock prices.
Positive changes in price will tend to be followed by negative changes. The

presence of reversal patterns will prevent variance from increasing proportionately with the return interval.

To see this, consider that if stock prices had *momentum,* rather than reversals, a gain would tend to be followed by another gain, a loss by another loss. Prices potentially could fluctuate over a wide range if you observe the stock over longer periods—*or if you measure the cumulative return over longer periods.*

With inertia, variance increases more than proportionately with the return interval. The variance of annual returns should be *more* than 12 times the variance of monthly returns.[47]

On the other hand, with reversals, gains tend to be corrected by losses, which narrows the possible range of performance if you observe, or compute the return, over longer periods of time.

In the presence of overreactive traders and reversal patterns, the variance increases *less than* proportionately with the length of the return interval. The annual variance should be less than 12 times the monthly variance.

Makhija and Nachtmann compute the variance of their stocks before cross-listing, using intervals ranging from 5 to 45 days to compute the return. For each interval, they compute a variance ratio, which is the variance as computed over the n-day interval divided by n times the stock's daily variance.

Thus, they would begin by computing each stock's variance over a 5-day interval, and then they would divide this variance by five times the stock's daily variance. If the ratio is less than 1.00, we have evidence of reversals in the pattern of returns. The average variance ratio across all the stocks, prior to cross-listing, is presented as the solid line in Figure 1.8.

Note that we observe some evidence of statistically insignificant momentum in the very short term. (The variance ratios are greater than 1.00.) However, as we go to intervals in excess of 25 days, we see evidence of overreaction and reversals. (The variance ratios are now less than 1.00.)

Now look at the *broken* curve. This curve shows the variance ratios *after* cross-listing.

The variance ratios are all *lower* than before.

Clearly indicating the presence of stronger reversal patterns, which can be associated with *more* correcting of overreactive pricing.

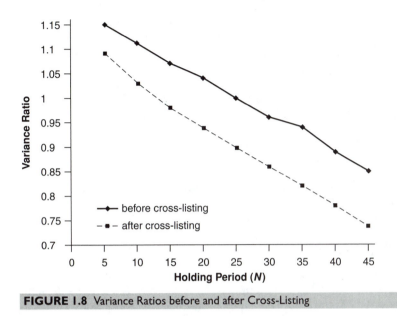

FIGURE 1.8 Variance Ratios before and after Cross-Listing

This seems odd *if the market is simply overreacting to pieces of information coming in from the real world.* All that has happened between the two curves is that we have given investors 5 hours of additional time to overreact.[48]

But what if the market is not merely overreacting to *real-world* information? What if it is overreacting to *itself?* Overreacting to its *own* price changes.

Then the 5 hours of additional trading time will give the market that much more information to overreact to. This seems to be a more plausible explanation for the striking results of Figure 1.8.

We see the tracks of THE BEAST in this figure. It *does* live inside the stock exchange, but when a firm's stock goes global, THE BEAST travels the world!

Taking Stock Again

It's time, once again, to take stock of what we have learned thus far.

- Stock volatility is too big and too unstable.
- When volatility goes up, stock prices go down, so as to increase the size of the risk premium in the market's aggregate future expected returns.
- The size of the price reaction increases with the size of the volatility shift.
- Most of the largest changes in price and volatility are unconnected to real-world events.

- When the number of trading hours per week declines, stock volatility goes down; when the number of trading hours increases, stock volatility goes up.
- When the number of trading hours per week rises, evidence of short-term overreaction becomes more pronounced.

By the way, do you see *any* good reason why MN's paper is locked away in a filing cabinet in Pittsburgh, Pennsylvania?

Papers locked away in filing cabinets don't have to be dealt with or responded to.

THE SIXTH MYSTERY: THE CASE OF THE VANISHING VOLATILITY

More Debt, Less Risk?

Highly leveraged transactions such as leveraged buyouts (LBOs) and leveraged recapitalizations were very popular in the 1980s. An interesting and largely overlooked feature of these types of transactions is that they are associated with a *reduction* of the risk of the firm as a whole. You might ask: "How can this be? I would think that a heavy use of debt in a transaction would *increase* risk, not *reduce* it."

According to modern finance, the amount of debt in a firm's capital determines the sharing of total firm risk among the capital contributors. With more debt and less stock, the firm's few remaining stockholders will bear the lion's share of the risk. Given the fixed nature of the debt claim and the residual nature of the stock claim, we would expect that the stock, standing last in the line of claims to profits, would be highly volatile indeed.

Unless there's some connection to the management of the firm's assets, however, the amount of debt employed in financing shouldn't materially affect the *aggregate* risk of *all* the firm's claims—debt as well as equity.

The distribution of risk among the claims in highly leveraged transactions was recently investigated by Kaplan and Stein,[49] professors from the University of Chicago and Massachusetts Institute of Technology, respectively.

Leverage and Beta: Theory

Kaplan and Stein measure risk by beta. The beta factor for a security (stock or bond) measures the sensitivity of its returns to changes in the returns to the market index. Figure 1.9 plots the rate of return to the security on the vertical scale. Rates of return to the market index are plotted on the horizontal scale. Each point on the diagram represents a pair of returns to the security and to

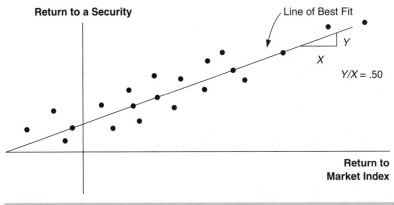

FIGURE 1.9 Beta Is the Slope of the Line of Best Fit

the index over a particular period of time—say, a month. A line of best fit is passed through the scatter plot. The slope of this line is the beta factor for the security. This particular security has a beta of .50. This means that if the return to the market index was to increase by 1%, we would expect the return to the security to rise by half that, or 0.5%.

Kaplan and Stein do a good job of explaining the effect of increasing financial leverage on beta:

> Imagine that XYZ Corp. is initially all equity-financed. And has a market value of $100 and an equity beta of 1.00. Now suppose that XYZ undertakes a recap, borrowing $85 from the bank and lower-grade bond lenders, and using the cash to pay an $85 dividend to shareholders. If there are no taxes or other sources of gains, the total market value of the company must still be $100. Thus, the "stub" equity component is worth $15. If the post re-capitalization debt has no systematic risk (beta), and then conservation of systematic risk implies that the stub equity must have a new beta of 6.67—the asset beta of 1.00 divided by the smaller equity to total capital ratio of 0.15. Suppose, however, that we measure the stub's beta and find it to be only 2.22, or one-third of 6.67. This must mean that the remaining two-thirds of total company risk is now borne by the debt-holders. If so, the debt has an implied beta of 0.78—the missing .67 of the asset beta divided by the 0.85 ratio of debt to total capital.[50]

If the debt has a beta of 0.78 and the stock has a beta of 2.22, the weighted average beta of all the claims will be 1.00—the original beta of the firm's assets.

$$\text{Asset Beta} = \% \text{ Equity} \times \text{Equity Beta} + \% \text{ Debt} \times \text{Debt Beta}$$
$$1.00 \quad = \quad .15 \quad \times \quad 2.22 \quad + \quad .85 \quad \times \quad .78$$

We see that, when the risk of the assets stays constant (in this case at 1.00), if a company reduced its equity while increasing its debt, its equity beta should rise dramatically unless there is a significant increase in the beta of its debt.

Leverage and Beta: Reality

Kaplan and Stein study 12 companies that recapitalized, moving from mostly equity to mostly debt, in the years 1985 through 1988. The characteristics of the 12 companies, before and after the transactions, are shown in Table 1.9. We see that, on average, the firms went from an average of 74% equity in their capital structures to only 15.5%.

KS compute the betas for the stocks using daily data over the 6 months prior to the recap announcement. They find that the firms have an average beta of 1.01 during this period. Next, they compute the betas in the 6 months following the completion of the recap. The betas now average 1.38. Naturally, there is an increase, but not nearly the increase that KS expected. In fact, the betas of four of the companies actually went down!

Table 1.10 shows the risk of these firms before and after the leveraged transactions. The pre-recap *asset* betas are computed using the equation above, the pre- and post-recap percentages for equity and debt, the statistical

TABLE 1.9   Pre- and Post-Recapitalization Capital Structures for 12 Leveraged Recapitalizations Completed from 1985 to 1988

		Pre-recapitalization			
Company	Recap Completed	Debt (%)	Preferred (%)	Common (%)	Total Capital ($M)
1. Colt Industries	10/08/86	11.3	0.0	88.7	1,527
2. FMC	05/29/86	14.6	0.0	85.6	1,916
3. Fruehauf	12/24/86	41.6	0.0	58.4	1,245
4. Harcourt Brace Jovanovich	07/28/87	27.7	0.0	72.3	2,488
5. Holiday	04/22/87	49.5	0.0	50.5	2,640
6. Interco	12/23/88	26.6	0.0	73.4	2,083
7. Kroger	12/05/88	28.7	6.1	65.2	4099
8. Multimedia	10/02/85	8.6	0.0	91.4	611
9. Owens Corning Fiberglass	11/06/86	27.2	0.0	72.8	2,085
10. Shoney's	08/04/88	1.7	0.0	98.3	762
11. Swank	03/01/88	31.9	0.0	68.0	83
12. USG	07/14/88	37.0	0.0	63.0	2,301
Average		25.5	0.5	74.0	1,824
Median		27.5	0.0	72.5	2,025

estimates of equity beta, and an assumption that the debt betas are all equal to 0.15.[51]

Note the numbers for the post-recap *asset* betas. They are also computed using the equation above, the computed equity beta for the post-recap period, and an assumption that the beta for the debt is zero.

Examine this table carefully. Note that, *in each and every case,* the risk of these firms went down *substantially.* On average, the risk associated with the assets of these firms falls to *less than a third* of its value prior to the recap.

Something very interesting happened to the risk of these firms. It disappeared!

Where did it go?

Are the Bonds Bearing the Risk?

To try to explain the puzzle, Kaplan and Stein make the rather bold assumption that the recaps result in a reduction in the *fixed* costs to the firm.[52] In fact, they assume that all the increase in firm value observed in the vicinity of the recap

TABLE 1.9   *(continued)*

			Post-recapitalization	
Company	*Recap Completed*	*Debt (%)*	*Preferred (%)*	*Common (%)*	*Total Capital ($M)*
1. Colt Industries	10/08/86	84.0	0.0	16.0	2,103
2. FMC	05/29/86	74.4	0.0	25.6	2,554
3. Fruehauf	12/24/86	83.6	13.9	2.6	1,916
4. Harcourt Brace Jovanovich	07/28/87	70.2	13.0	16.7	3,656
5. Holiday	04/22/87	88.2	0.0	11.8	3,364
6. Interco	12/23/88	84.7	11.2	4.1	2,955
7. Kroger	12/05/88	87.8	0.0	12.2	6,286
8. Multimedia	10/02/85	81.1	0.0	18.9	1,115
9. Owens Corning Fiberglass	11/06/86	84.3	0.0	15.7	2,929
10. Shoney's	08/04/88	72.9	0.0	27.1	1,041
11. Swank	03/01/88	74.8	0.0	25.2	94
12. USG	07/14/88	89.4	0.0	10.6	3,495
Average		81.3	3.2	15.5	2,626
Median		83.8	0.0	15.9	2,742

Source: Kaplan, S., and J. Stein, "How Risky Is the Debt in Highly Leveraged Transactions?" *Journal of Financial Economics,* September 1990, p. 220.

TABLE 1.10 Risk before and after Recapitalization for 12 Leveraged Recapitalizations Completed from 1985 to 1988

Company	Pre-recapitalization		Post-recapitalization	
	Equity Beta	*Implicit Asset Beta*	*Equity Beta*	*Implicit Asset Beta*
1. Colt Industries	0.63	0.57	1.29	0.21
2. FMC	0.88	0.77	1.09	0.28
3. Fruehauf	0.76	0.51	0.73	0.12
4. Harcourt Brace Jovanovich	1.85	1.38	1.68	0.50
5. Holiday	0.75	0.46	1.65	0.20
6. Interco	0.93	0.72	1.96	0.30
7. Kroger	1.20	0.90	1.41	0.17
8. Multimedia	0.75	0.70	1.22	0.23
9. Owens Corning Fiberglass	1.10	0.84	1.86	0.29
10. Shoney's	0.76	0.75	1.45	0.39
11. Swank	1.14	0.83	0.84	0.21
12. USG	1.37	0.92	1.36	0.14
Average	1.01	0.78	1.38	0.25
Median	0.91	0.76	1.38	0.22

Source: Kaplan S., and J. Stein, "How Risky Is the Debt in Highly Leveraged Transactions?" *Journal of Financial Economics,* September 1990, p. 228.

can be attributed to a fixed cost reduction that reduces the firm's *asset* betas proportionately.[53]

Assuming that this is the case, we get a revised set of numbers in Table 1.11.

Same basic result. Where did the risk go? Perhaps it's being borne by the firm's bondholders. However, as we shall see, the bonds of these firms simply don't carry that much systematic risk.[54]

Kaplan and Stein can get weekly prices for the bonds of eight of their companies. They compute the betas of these bonds directly, by statistically relating their returns to the returns to the market index in the manner of Figure 1.9. The estimated betas are displayed in Table 1.12 along with the debt betas needed to keep asset risk intact. The implied debt betas are those required to keep the risk of the assets "intact" under two assumptions: (a) the recap lowers fixed costs and (b) it does not.[55]

If the bonds of these firms are found to carry substantial levels of systematic risk, then we will have found the missing risk—imbedded in the bond returns.

| | Pre-recapitalization | | Post-recapitalization | |
	Equity Beta	Asset Beta Adjusted	Equity Beta	Asset Beta
TABLE 1.11 Risk before and after Recapitalization, Assuming Total Market-Adjusted Premium Represents Reduction in Fixed Costs for 12 Leveraged Recapitalizations Completed from 1985 to 1988				
Company				
1. Colt Industries	0.63	0.42	1.29	0.21
2. FMC	0.88	0.70	1.09	0.28
3. Fruehauf	0.76	0.36	0.73	0.12
4. Harcourt Brace Jovanovich	1.85	0.96	1.68	0.50
5. Holiday	0.75	0.40	1.65	0.20
6. Interco	0.93	0.55	1.96	0.30
7. Kroger	1.20	0.59	1.41	0.17
8. Multimedia	0.75	0.40	1.22	0.23
9. Owens Corning Fiberglass	1.10	0.61	1.86	0.29
10. Shoney's	0.76	0.63	1.45	0.39
11. Swank	1.14	0.65	0.84	0.21
12. USG	1.37	0.65	1.36	0.14
Average	1.01	0.58	1.38	0.25
Median	0.91	0.60	1.38	0.22

Source: Kaplan S., and J. Stein, "How Risky Is the Debt in Highly Leveraged Transactions?" *Journal of Financial Economics,* September 1990, p. 231–232.

However, Table 1.12 clearly shows that the actual risk of the bonds is insufficient to account for the missing risk. For the risk of the total firms to be constant across the recap, the risk of the new bonds would have to be approximately two to four times what the statistical estimate of the bonds' risk actually turn out to be.

Who Stole the Risk?

What happened here? Twelve companies decide to dramatically increase the amount of debt in their capital structures. Bonds are simply exchanged for stock. Remarkably, in each and every case, the companies behind these securities become less risky.

Much less risky.

The total risk of the firms is cut by *one-half* to *two-thirds,* depending on what you assume about fixed costs.[56]

Why?

TABLE 1.12   Direct Lower-Grade Debt Beta Estimates and Implicit Debt Betas

	DIRECT BETA ESTIMATES	IMPLICIT BETA ESTIMATES	
		Constant Asset Risk	*Reduced Asset Risk*
Company	*Beta of Bonds*	*Lower-grade*	*Lower-grade*
1. Colt Industries	0.30	0.59	0.34
2. FMC	0.26	0.90	0.77
3. Fruehauf	0.18	0.65	0.40
4. Holiday	0.60	0.35	0.28
5. Interco	−0.21	0.70	0.42
6. Kroger	0.24	1.17	0.68
7. Owens Corning Fiberglas	0.32	0.84	0.49
8. USG	0.30	1.16	0.75
Average	0.21	0.80	0.52
Median	0.28	0.77	0.46

Source: Kaplan, S., and J. Stein, "How Risky Is the Debt in Highly Leveraged Transactions?" *Journal of Financial Economics,* September 1990, p. 242.

If you can answer the following question, then you will know.

How big is THE BEAST that lives in the bond market?

THE SEVENTH MYSTERY: STOCKS SELLING CHEAP— THE STRANGE BEHAVIOR OF CLOSED-END INVESTMENT COMPANIES

What Is a Closed-End Fund?

Closed-end investment companies are similar to mutual funds. The basic difference between the two is how you buy or sell them. With a mutual fund, you buy and sell shares from the mutual fund itself at the net asset value of the fund (the total market value of all its investments divided by the number of shares that the fund has outstanding). You buy shares in a closed-end investment company as you would buy shares in any common stock—by sending your broker to the stock exchange or wherever the fund is traded to buy them from another investor who wants to sell them.

The closed-end fund is, therefore, priced in the market like any other stock.

You would think that valuing this stock would be a "lay-up," even for the *inefficient* market. After all, the total market value of the investments owned by the fund is reported weekly in the financial press.

It seems, however, that the stock market has a difficult time even sinking lay-ups.

The Discount

Think of this. You decide to form your own closed-end fund. Your Uncle Louie is an investment banker, and he is willing to help you sell a $1 million block of stock for no fee. Louie floats a million shares at $1.00 per share. Fortunately, Aunt Emma is a stock broker, and she's going to let you buy shares of stock for free. So you have her buy $1 million of AT&T. The shares of your new closed-end investment company are being traded on the New York Stock Exchange.

A few days later, you check the price of AT&T and find that it has increased slightly. At the same time, you check the price of your closed-end fund and find that it has gone *down*. The price has dropped from $1.00 per share to $.80! Your fund is now selling at a *discount*.

Much to your consternation, although the magnitude of the discount changes from day to day, your fund continues, on average, to sell at a bargain price.

Puzzled, you call a financial consultant to ask why. The consultant gives you several possible explanations.

First, he says, "You may be charging too much for your services as the manager in the fund."

"What's too much?" you ask.

"More than your value-added as a stock picker and portfolio manager," he says.

"But my salary is tiny relative to the size of the discount, and my salary doesn't change from day to day, but the discount does. Besides, I've checked into it, and I don't see any relationship between the size of the discounts on different funds and their expense ratios."[57]

The consultant offers another explanation. "Well, some closed-end funds invest in privately placed securities, which aren't very liquid. They may appraise the value of their illiquid investments too high in computing net asset values."

You reply: "Look. I only own AT&T. Is that liquid enough? Besides, I see lots of other funds out there holding only liquid investments, and they're selling at discounts too."

Backing into a corner, the consultant offers up yet another explanation. "Well, maybe you've got an accrued capital gain on your investment. Any new investor who buys your fund now would be buying into a tax liability right from the start."

But this also doesn't seem plausible. You've noticed that AT&T *has* gone up a bit, but not nearly enough to explain the size of the discount. Besides, you've noticed that the size of the discount gets *larger* when stock prices go *down* and *smaller* when they go *up*. If the tax argument held water, the opposite would happen.

So you fire your consultant, and continue on, still perplexed.

The Discount as an Index of Investor Sentiment

Don't feel bad. Financial economists have puzzled over these discounts for a *long time*.

Recently, however, three professors named Lee, Shleifer, and Thaler (LST) have shed some light on the issue.[58]

They studied 20 closed-end funds in the period 1965 through 1985. They collect monthly net asset values for the funds. Then they calculate the size of the monthly discounts on each fund. The individual monthly discounts are then aggregated, based on the total size of each fund, to form a *discount index*.

The behavior of the discount index over time is shown in Figure 1.10. The number of new funds started in each year is also shown in the figure. We see that the discount is highly variable over time, and new funds tend to be formed when the discount is relatively small.

The latter finding implies that the discounts on individual funds tend to be positively correlated. LST find that, in fact, they are, with an average correlation coefficient between funds being .53.

These researchers offer the hypothesis that, *since the magnitude of the discount is both big and variable over time,* investing in a closed-end fund is more risky than a direct investment in the portfolio of stocks owned by the fund. Because of this, risk-averse investors want a higher expected return on the fund. The only way to get a higher return in the future is to discount the price of the fund today.

They take the size of the discount to be an index of *investor sentiment* about future returns on closed-end funds and other securities.[59] They predict that, as investors become more optimistic, security prices overall will go up. With increased

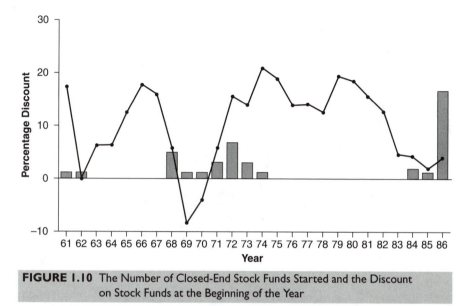

FIGURE 1.10 The Number of Closed-End Stock Funds Started and the Discount on Stock Funds at the Beginning of the Year

Source: Lee, C., A. Shleifer, and R. Thaler, "Investor Sentiment and the Closed-End Fund Puzzle," *Journal of Finance,* March, 1991, p. 80.

pessimism, they should go down. Taking the discount index as a barometer of investor sentiment, there should be a negative relationship between changes in the size of the discount index and rates of return to stocks in general.

An *increase* in the size of the discount index should mean *lower* returns to common stocks.

Lee, Shleifer, and Thaler rank the stocks in their study by the size of the company. Then they form the stocks into equally weighted size deciles. Figure 1.11 shows the sensitivities of stock returns to changes in the value of the discount index. These "betas" relate changes in the discount index to stock returns to different portfolios of common stocks. All of the betas are statistically significant at very high levels of confidence.

The beta for the smallest stocks is –0.67. How to interpret this? Note from Figure 1.10, that the size of the discount fell by about 18 percentage points in the first year. Given the beta for the smallest decile in Figure 1.11, we would expect the returns to these stocks to be 12 percentage points higher because of what happened to the discount index.

A substantial effect. And we see that the effect becomes smaller as we go from the smallest stocks to the largest.[60]

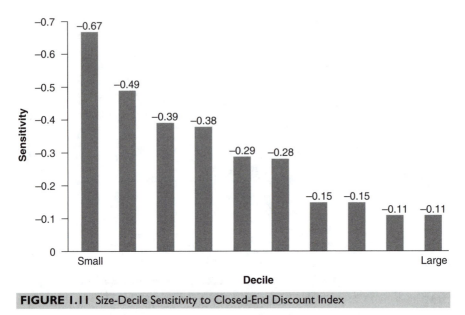

FIGURE 1.11 Size-Decile Sensitivity to Closed-End Discount Index

Source: Adapted from Lee, C., A. Shleifer, and R. Thaler, "Investor Sentiment and the Closed-End Fund Puzzle," *Journal of Finance,* March, 1991.

Do you remember the study by French and Roll?

They find that volatility was 50 times larger for small stocks when the exchange was open—but only 12 times larger for large stocks.

THE BEAST has a bigger impact on small companies.[61]

The Final Inventory

Let's itemize what we've learned one last time:

- Stock volatility is much too big and much too unstable.
- When volatility goes up, stock prices go down, apparently to increase the size of the risk premium in the market's aggregate future expected returns.
- The size of the price reaction increases with the size of the volatility shift.
- In the market's history, most of the largest changes in price and in volatility are unrelated to real-world events.
- When the number of trading hours per week gets smaller (exchange holidays), stock volatility goes down; when the number of trading hours gets larger (cross-listing), stock volatility and short-term reversal patterns become more pronounced.
- When more debt is issued, firm risk decreases.
- The discounts on closed-end funds become larger when the stock returns get smaller.

None of these effects are small. They are all *major* anomalies. And they all can be explained in a single stroke.

Notes

1. A line of best fit is the unique line passed through the scatter such that the *sum* of the squared vertical distances of each plot point from the line is *minimized*.

2. The slope of the line of best fit is given by: the product of (a) the volatility of the perfect forecast price and (b) the correlation between the two prices divided by the volatility of the market price. As discussed earlier, if the market is efficient, the slope for the relationship between changes in the Perfect Foresight Price and changes in the market price should be 1.00. This being the case, the ratio of the volatility of the market price to the volatility of the Perfect Foresight Price should equal the correlation coefficient between the two. (For the original derivation, see R. Shiller, 1981, "Do Stock Prices Move Too Much to Be Justified by Subsequent Changes in Dividends?" *American Economic Review,* pp. 421–435.)

3. See R. Shiller, *Market Volatility* (Cambridge, MA: MIT Press, 1990), p. 78. Also see S. LeRoy and R. Porter, 1981, "The Present Value Relation: Tests Based on Implied Variance Bounds," *Econometrica,* pp. 555–574.

4. Shiller assumes that the present value of dividends to be received after 1988 is equal to the 1988 price.

5. R. Shiller, *Market Volatility* (Cambridge MA: MIT Press, 1990), p. 82.

6. You may recall from the discussion that the perfect foresight pricing equation calls for real (inflation-adjusted) discount rates. It is likely that the real rate is more stable than the nominal commercial paper rate used by Shiller. Thus, Shiller's estimate of the volatility of the Perfect Foresight Price series is, for this reason, upward biased.

7. See M. Flavin, 1983, "Excess Volatility in the Financial Markets: A Reassessment of the Empirical Evidence," *Journal of Political Economy,* pp. 921–956; A. Kleidon, 1986, "Variance Bounds Tests and Stock Price Valuation Models," *Journal of Political Economy,* pp. 953–1001; and T. Marsh and R. Merton, 1986, "Dividend Variability and Variance Bounds Tests for the Rationality of Stock Market Prices," *American Economic Review,* pp. 483–498.

8. Ackert and Smith argue that if all cash flows received by common shareholders are considered, stock prices are not too volatile to be explained by the discounted value of total cash flows. However, a very significant portion of their nondividend cash flows is payments received in corporate takeovers. This seems strange because Shiller argues that stock prices are too volatile relative to the cash flows from the operations of the firm. Many takeovers are motivated by assessments that the assets of the target are undervalued. Apparently, Ackert and Smith feel there is a fundamental difference between noncorporate investors driving an undervalued stock up in price and a corporate raider doing the same thing. In the case of the former, it is seen as a part of the excess volatility anomaly. In the case of the latter, it is seen as a volatile component of the cash flow that "resolves" the anomaly. Regardless, nondividend "cash flows" have been of significant size relative to dividends only in the last two decades. Are we to conclude that their appearance has resolved the excess volatility problem documented over the century? Is the stock market to be seen as too volatile (and therefore inefficient) in the first 8 decades of the century and not too volatile (and therefore efficient) over the last

2? See L. Ackert, and B. Smith, 1993, "Stock Price Volatility, Ordinary Dividends, and Other Cash Flows to Shareholder," *Journal of Finance,* pp. 1147–1160.

9. The market's assessment of its own volatility can be obtained by observing the relationship between the cash price for the S&P 100 Stock Index and the corresponding price for options written on the index. The most important determinant of the value of those options is the volatility of the index. Given the terms of the option (exercise price and maturity), the level of the risk-free rate, and the prices of the options and the index, it is possible to back out the level of index volatility that is consistent with the option price at any given point in time. Based on this methodology, we can say that there was about a 7-fold increase in volatility in the week between Monday the twelfth and Monday the nineteenth. See R. A. Haugen, E. Talmor, and W. Torous, "The Effect of Volatility Changes on the Level of Stock Prices and Subsequent Expected Return," *Journal of Finance,* July, 1991, pp. 985–1007.

10. HTT pass two contiguous blocks of time through their series of daily percentage changes in the market index. Each block spans 4 weeks. Call the first block the "leading block" and the block following behind the "trailing block." They calculate the variance (the square of the volatility) of the daily percentage changes in each block. At any given point in time, they take the ratio of the variance 4 weeks ahead to the variance 4 weeks behind. As we move the blocks forward toward a volatility increase, the leading block will begin to enter the high-volatility period. The variance of the leading block will begin to grow, as will the variance ratio. The ratio reaches its peak when the leading block is fully into the event and the trailing block is fully out of it. As we continue to move forward, the trailing block enters the event, and the variance in the denominator of the ratio begins to increase as well. The variance ratio now begins to fall, leaving its *peak* as the identifier of the time-incidence of the beginning of the volatility event.

    HTT run the moving blocks through their time-series of percentage changes in the market index from 1897 through 1988. When the variance ratio reaches a level at which they can say with 99% confidence that there has been an upward or downward shift in volatility, HTT mark the spot and begin looking for the peak or the trough in the ratio that marks the beginning of the event. (See D. Wichern and R. Miller, 1976, "Changes in Variance in First-Order Autoregressive Time-Series Models—With an Application," *Journal of the Royal Statistical Association,* pp. 248–256.)

11. This result is reinforced by Black, who finds a negative relationship between stock returns and changes in volatility. It is also confirmed by the results of French, Schwert, and Stambaugh, and by those of Duffee, who finds that changes in volatility are negatively related to stock returns. See F. Black, "Studies of Stock Price Volatility Changes," *Proceedings of the 1976 Meetings of the American Statistical Association, Business and Economics Section,* pp. 177–181. Also see K. French, W. Schwert, and R. Stambaugh, 1987, "Expected Stock Returns and Volatility," *Journal of Financial Economics,* pp. 3–29, and G. Duffee, 1995, "Stock Returns and Volatility: A Firm Level Analysis," *Journal of Financial Economics,* pp. 399–420.

12. In a differently designed test, French, Schwert, and Stambaugh show that the rate of return to the market index in any given month is negatively related to the unexpected change in market volatility during the month. See K. French, W. Schwert, and R. Stambaugh, 1987 *Journal of Financial Economics,* pp. 3–29.

13. This dramatic evidence in support of a high level of risk aversion on the part of stock market investors stands in marked contrast to the evidence coming from the *cross-section* of stock market returns. There is very little evidence that stocks of relatively greater risk carry relatively greater expected returns. At the least, we can say that relatively risky stocks have failed to produce relatively greater returns for their investors for the past 40 years! A possible explanation for disparity in the evidence coming from the time-series and the cross-section is provided in R. Haugen, *The New Finance: The Case Against Efficient Markets* (Englewood Cliffs, NJ: Prentice Hall, 1995).

14. We would expect investors to require higher (lower) returns only over the period for which the volatility shift is expected to persist. Because, as we have discussed above, volatility shifts occur quite often, the expected duration of the shift is likely to be short. A 4-week period to measure the realization of the new expected return seems reasonable, and it has the advantage of being consistent with the periods of the other blocks.

15. Remember that this is only the average percentage change in the price of the index. Adding the dividend yield brings the return to a level roughly commensurate with yields on fixed income securities over the period of the study.

16. As measured by the change in the volatility implied by the market value of the options on the S&P 100 Stock Index and the value of the S&P 500 Index itself.

17. This estimate is made after excluding the crash from the events used to measure the relationship between the magnitude of the volatility shift and the magnitude of the corresponding price response.

18. In a portfolio insurance strategy, you automatically sell stocks from your portfolio into a market decline. On the eve of October 19, as much as $80 billion in equities was invested this way. One large pension plan, which had invested under the strategy, accounted for 7% of the total volume of trading on the nineteenth, as it repeatedly sold $100 million blocks of stock in the cash market.

19. The media search is conducted for the last day of the first block as well as for all the days of the second block. The search was conducted using *Day by Day, Facts on File,* and *Keesing's Contemporary Archives.*

20. In their individual presidential addresses to the American Finance Association, Fisher Black and Richard Roll have focused on the extremely low power of economic fundamentals and empirical models in explaining changes in stock prices. See F. Black, 1986, "Noise," *Journal of Finance,* pp. 529–543; and R. Roll, 1988, "R^2", *Journal of Finance,* pp. 541–566.

21. D. Cutler, J. Poterba, and L. Summers, 1989, *Journal of Portfolio Management,* pp. 4–12.

22. They use the Cowles Index for the early years of their work, and then they switch to the S&P 500.

23. The unexplained change in the variable after relating it to lagged changes in its own value as well as to lagged changes in the other economic/financial variables.

24. The "T" statistic on the volatility variable is –7.33.

25. All the events were carried by the *New York Times* as the lead story and were indicated in the Business Section as having affected stock market participants.

26. Assuming that daily market returns are normally distributed.

27. Similarly, Schwert finds that the volatility of stock returns is not significantly related to the volatility of other economic variables such as the long- and short-term interest rates, the money supply, and inflation rates. See G. W. Schwert, 1989,

"Why Does Stock Market Volatility Change Over Time?" *Journal of Finance,* pp. 1115–1153.

28. Another possible cause would be significant changes in the relative prices of competitive beverages, but Roll allows for this in some of his tests.

29. See R. Roll, 1984, "Orange Juice and Weather," *American Economic Review,* pp. 861–880.

30. That means the expected percentage change in the price tomorrow has nothing to do with the change in the price today or any other day in the past.

31. See K. French and R. Roll, 1986, "Stock Return Variances: The Arrival of Information and the Reaction of Traders," *Journal of Financial Economics,* pp. 5–26.

32. Since the variance over n hours is n times the hourly variance, it will be true that the ratio of the variance over the 72 hours on Saturday through Monday to the 24 hours on other days can be written as:

$$\frac{66 \times \text{Variance}(C) + 6 \times \text{Variance}(O)}{18 \times \text{Variance}(C) + 6 \times \text{Variance}(O)} = 1.11$$

where Variance (C) and Variance (O) are the variance when the market is closed and open, respectively. By manipulating the equation, we can solve for Variance (O)/ Variance (C).

33. To test whether the exchange holiday effect is real, French and Roll look at the variance of Wednesday–Thursday returns for each year *except* 1968 relative to the 1-day weekday variance for the entire period of their study (July 1963 through December 1982). They find that the average ratio across all the years is 2.00—just as it should be. (The ratios over the individual years ranged from a low of 1.18 to a high of 4.32.) They conclude that the 1968 variance ratio of 1.14 was not caused by chance but rather by the exchange holiday.

34. For exchange holidays, the ratio of the 2-day variance (the exchange holiday and the day following) to the 1-day variance on an open day is equal to:

$$\frac{24 \times \text{Variance}(C) + 6 \times \text{Variance}(O) + 18 \times \text{Variance}(C)}{6 \times \text{Variance}(O) + 18 \times \text{Variance}(C)} = 1.145$$

The ratio for the open to closed variance can be computed as 25.

35. For election holidays, the open volatility is estimated to be 21 times the closed volatility.

36. After seeing the exchange holiday results, French and Roll eventually narrow the explanation for their results to two alternatives. The first is that return variances are higher during trading hours because most private information is incorporated into prices during this period. They say, for example, that most security analysts are at work at this time, visiting corporate headquarters and reading company documents. They conjecture that analysts might be more likely to look for private information during trading hours because they can quickly act on it, and therefore it is more valuable. Presumably, they stop looking during exchange holidays for this reason. The second possible explanation they consider is that the high trading-time volatility is caused by pricing errors that occur during trading.

To discriminate between these competing hypotheses, French and Roll look at the ratio of the weekly variance during exchange holiday weeks relative to the variance over other weeks. They find that the exchange holiday variance is 82% as large as the variance over the other weeks. (Presumably because 1 out of the normal 5 trading days is missing.) They agree that this would support the pricing error hypothesis because private information found during the holiday, or found after the holiday because of the search delay, would be impounded into prices on the following Thursday and Friday, increasing the variance then, raising the weekly variance ratio toward 100%.

They also argue that if the results are caused by pricing errors when the exchange is open there should be evidence of short-term reversal patterns in stock returns as the errors are subsequently corrected. French and Roll look for these reversal patterns, *and they find them, and state that they have found them.*

As a final discriminatory test, these researchers state that pricing errors are likely to be corrected within 3 weeks. This being the case, the variance of long holding-period returns is less likely to be affected by pricing errors than the variance of short holding-period returns. Confirming that this is in fact the case, they find that the "semi-annualized" variance of daily returns is significantly greater than the variance of 6-month returns. And the same result holds for periods shorter than 6 months. Amazingly, in spite of *all* this evidence supporting the pricing errors hypothesis, French and Roll, long-standing supporters of the Efficient Market Hypothesis, conclude, at the end of their paper, that the *exchange holiday variances suggest that private information cause most stock price changes. WOW!*

37. In the Seventh Mystery, we will find a stronger relationship between the returns on small stocks and changes in the magnitude of the closed-end investment company discounts.

38. A. Makhija, and R. Nachtmann, 1989, "Empirical Evidence on Alternative Theories of Stock Return Variances: The Effect of Expanded Trading Time on NYSE-LSE Cross-listed Stocks," unpublished manuscript, University of Pittsburgh.

39. Firms are included in the study if there are no missing rates of return for the 400 trading days surrounding the cross-listing and if the firm does not merge with another during this period.

40. Firm sizes were computed as of the date of the cross-listing admission to the LSE.

41. During the period of their study, the LSE was open from 4:30 A.M. to 10:30 A.M., EST, and the NYSE was open from 9:30 A.M. to 3:30 P.M., EST.

42. For the average, the increase in the daily variance is consistent with an increase in the annualized volatility from 36% to 41%.

43. Wilcoxon Z matched-pair tests provide strong support for the hypothesis that the distribution of the variance after cross-listing is fundamentally different from the distribution before cross-listing. No contraindicative inferences from parametric findings were observed.

44. The average changes in the variances of the 30 stocks in the Dow Jones Industrial Average are netted from the changes in the cross-listed stocks, matched in calendar time.

45. Interestingly, Makhija and Nachtmann find no significant increase in the market beta factors (the sensitivity of individual stock return to market return). The significant increases come from increases in the fraction of the stock's variance that is unexplained by the market—the stock's so-called residual variance. This makes sense because, if the increases in variance are created by additional pricing errors being made by London traders, these errors are being made during time periods when the U.S. market index isn't visibly moving. The U.S. market is closed during these periods—reducing the possibility that London traders are reacting to contemporary moves in the U.S. stock index. Indeed, they may be, instead, reacting to changes in the UK stock index.

46. French and Roll offer the Preposterous Private Information Hypothesis as a possible explanation, for why the variance is anywhere from 13 to 100 times larger when the exchange is open than when it is closed. They argue that traders are more apt to look for private information when open because they can act on it more quickly. I must say, after working with, interviewing, lecturing, and talking to money managers for more than 21 years, that I have never seen anyone behaving in this manner.

47. I'm using months and years because a year unambiguously spans 12 times more time than an average month. Stock returns actually exhibit reversal patterns in the short term (1 to 2 months), inertial patterns in the intermediate term (6 to 12 months), and reversal patterns over the long term (3 to 5 years). Makhija and Nachtmann conduct their tests of variance ratios over the short term, where reversal patterns tend to be present.

48. There was 1 hour of overlap in the 6 hours of trading in New York and London.

49. S. Kaplan and J. Stein, 1990, "How Risky Is the Debt in Highly Leveraged Transactions?" *Journal of Financial Economics,* pp. 215–245.

50. *Ibid.,* pp. 217 and 218.

51. This is approximately equal to the beta on Treasury bonds over their sample period.

52. Fixed costs are those that should not be expected to change in the short term with changes in the level of the firm's production. Thus, executives, salaries would be considered to be a fixed cost and raw materials used in production would be considered a variable cost. If the recaps have the effect of reducing variable costs instead of fixed costs, then the risk of the firms should actually be expected to go *up*.

53. The pre-recap asset betas are adjusted downward by KS, based on the assumption that all of the increase in the market value of the firm, net of the corresponding increase in the market index, from 40 days before the recap announcement until the capitalization is complete, is attributable to a reduction in fixed costs, which would reduce the beta associated with the assets of the firms proportionately.

54. Systematic risk is that part of a securities volatility that is contributed to a well-diversified portfolio of which it is a member. The security's beta factor is a measure of that contribution.

55. The implicit betas displayed in Table 1.11 are for the marketable bonds issued by each firm. In calculating these betas, bank debt is assumed to have half the systematic risk of the marketable bonds.

56. As with the cases of reducing and extending the length of the trading day, the evidence is always more convincing if it can be shown that the effects work consistently in both directions. Kaplan and Stein show that increasing debt has the effect of *reducing* firm risk. Does increasing equity have the effect of *increasing* firm risk? Healy and Palepu find that company risk (again measured by beta) tends to increase after a primary issue of common stock. See P. Healy and K. Palepu, 1990, "Earnings and Risk Changes Surrounding Primary Stock Offers," *Journal of Accounting Research,* pp. 25–48.

57. See B. Malkiel, 1977, "The Valuation of Closed-End Investment Company Shares," *Journal of Finance,* pp. 847–859.

58. C. Lee, A. Shleifer, and R. Thaler, 1991, "Investor Sentiment and the Closed-End Fund Puzzle," *Journal of Finance,* pp. 75–109.

59. Oddly, Lee, Shleifer, and Thaler never fully explain why the discount, which they claim to be a manifestation of a risk premium, would serve as a barometer of investor optimism or pessimism. In this sense, they get the story only half right.

60. Some may argue that Lee, Shleifer, and Thaler get this result because closed-end investment companies tend to invest in small stocks. They argue that, if anything, the contrary is true. To show this, they perform the analysis of Figure 1.11 using the discount on a single closed-end fund, Tricontinental Corporation, as their index of investor sentiment. The results of this test are basically the same in spite of the fact that Tricontinental invests only in large stocks.

61. Swaminathan finds that increases in closed-end discounts forecast low real growth rates in gross domestic product, consumption, and after-tax corporate earnings. He indicates that this may mean that the discounts stem from something rational as opposed to investor sentiment. However, Bittlingmayer finds a negative relationship between volatility and economic growth. It may well be that increases in volatility increase the size of the discounts in the shorter term and slow down economic growth in the longer term. See B. Swaminathan, 1996, "Time-Varying Expected Small Firm Returns and Closed-End Fund Discounts," *Review of Financial Studies,* Fall, pp. 845–888. See also G. Bittlingmayer, "Output, Stock Volatility, and Political Uncertainty in a Natural Experiment: Germany, 1880–1940," working paper, Graduate School of Management, University of California, Davis, April 1997.

PART II

Nineteen-thirty

FAT CATS

From 1,000 feet, the summer sunset is magnificent. Gold fades to orange, orange to purple, purple to indigo.

Bisecting the fire in the gold is a stiletto of a building.

Now, Manhattan Island has many impressive buildings, but there is something about this one that makes it dominate. Not because it is the largest—at 100 stories there are four taller buildings in the neighborhood.

But this structure is particularly imposing. Its design is particularly striking. They sometimes call it "The Needle," an oval obelisk set on a rectangular base of black marble. The obelisk itself is a solid, jet-black mirror of one-way glass. No corners. No visible windows. No apparent seams.

Ominous and impenetrable.

Beyond its unusual design, The Needle dominates simply because of what it represents.

Its name is The Badsworth and Hyde Tower—home base of Badsworth and Hyde, by far the single largest investment banking firm in the world. It has been for some time, the very center of world financial power.

Above and to the right of The Needle, the planet Venus gradually reveals itself, adding a final touch to this incredibly beautiful panorama. As if to answer, lights begin to emerge from the obelisk. Lights, by the thousands, invisible in daylight, reveal themselves in the growing darkness.

The eyes of The Needle.

You can see them clearly now. Nevertheless, the eyes are *always* there—watching intently over their domain. Eyes seen, by the people they study, only at night.

Changing our vantage point, we move slowly toward the sunset, in a 180-degree arc around The Needle. Looking from the west, we see Central Park beyond the building, then the East River, and finally, in the distance, the lights of Queens and Long Island.

One of the eyes, near the top of the obelisk, is obviously bigger and brighter than all the others. It sits on the ninety-fifth floor, and it is the eye of Brighton Bellow, chairman of the board of Badsworth and Hyde (B&H). The light emerges from the vast expanse of his personal office.

On the eastern wall of this office are twin, 20-foot doors that lead directly to the enormous boardroom of the firm. A room 100 feet long and 60 feet wide. From the floor up, the first 10 feet are solid cherry, trimmed in intricate carvings depicting the history of American industry. Above the cherry base are 20-foot square panels of gray on white marble, each meticulously matched and framed in cherry. There are four of these panels on the two longer walls, and two more at each end of the room.

Centered within each of the panels are 15-foot portraits of the 10 men who served as Chairman of the firm's Board of Directors and who led B&H to its position of world power. At the far wall is Christian Badsworth, the founder of B&H back in 1836. It was then the First Commercial Bank of New York. Under Badsworth, the (then) commercial bank helped finance the likes of Jay Gould and Jim Fisk, railroad barons who laid track from one end of the country to the other. Badsworth passed the flag to John Kingston, and he, in turn, to the others who helped Carnegie make his fortune in steel and Rockefeller his in oil.

Directly over the door leading to the office of the present chairman is the cold, ominous face of Brighton Bellow, the last man to take the flag. It is Bellow who sits at the head of the 40-foot table where his directors periodically assemble for their meetings.

Bellow sits in his chair at the table head at this very moment. To his right is his probable successor and the current president of B&H, Logan Winslowe. To his left, the firm's chief economist, the well-known and highly regarded Whyte Hunter. The three men sit alone in the vast expanse.

It is the evening of August 27th, the first Monday following the adjournment of the Republican National Convention.

Bellow turns to Hunter. "Whyte, I asked you to meet with me today so we could discuss financial and economic conditions as they relate to the state of the campaign." Bellow opened a large, ornate silver box containing 100 of the finest Cuban cigars and offered one to Hunter. "Tell me what you think."

Hunter lights the cigar and replies, "Well, we've got a Republican candidate who thinks in terms of 'business as usual.' In a large sense, I sympathize with his position. With the obvious problems with the deficit and the weakness in economic activity, the stock market's pretty shaky right now. But supply-side economics is bound to work in the long run, so why dump it because of a temporary setback?"

"I'd have to admit that I agree with you. What about you, Logan?"

"You *know* I do, Chief. All we need right now is to have the Democrats get in the White House and screw up 8 years of carefully planned, solid economic progress."

Bellow turned once again to Hunter, "What about that Democrat and his proposal for a tax increase? What do you think of *that?*"

"Brighton, the Democrats are playing on the American public's concern for the budget deficit problem and its perceived connection to volatility in the stock market. Polls say the shaky economy is the number one problem facing America today. The Democrats know that. But, they also know that people don't like to write checks made out to the IRS. Never have; never will. But the deficit doesn't seem to be going away. The national debt once again looms as a threat for the American people and for their kids. People are really becoming concerned. Maybe just concerned enough to overcome their distaste for more taxes. Their campaign could work."

"But, you know as well as I, that strategy backfired in the last election. Besides, a tax increase just doesn't make any sense right now. Consumer confidence is down. Ever since the Second Great Crash, people have been cutting back on consumption because of paper losses in the stock market. A tax increase will mean further spending cuts. Could be just what's needed to send us into the next great depression."

Winslowe: "But listen, Chief. First of all, in the last election, the Democratic candidate was running against an extremely popular incumbent. I doubt very much if any strategy would have worked for him. Furthermore, I just don't think people are thinking in terms of the depressing effects of a tax increase. Their minds are on the *stock market;* it really seems to be concerning people."

Hunter's eyebrows rose. "The problem is not with the *stock market.* There's *nothing* wrong with the *stock market.* The volatility is simply a reflection of the prevailing uncertainty in the *economy."*

Bellow pondered Hunter's comment. "Maybe so. Maybe so. . . . Still, if the stock market's okay, I don't see how you can explain the *30% drop in prices* that we had back on the 6th of June. . . . In any case, what happens if the Democrats win? Do you agree that a tax increase is likely to pull the plug on the economy? And beyond that, what do you see as the implications for B&H and for the rest of the investment banking business?"

"I think that, *basically,* you're pretty much on target, Brighton. A tax hike would really be bad news right now. As for the business, firms are already cutting back drastically on their capital spending. You know what that means— less investing means less financing and that's bad news for all of us. On the plus side, however, the higher level of market volatility means more volume, and since we've cornered the market on trading, that should go a long way toward softening the blow. By the way, don't let the Second Great Crash shake your faith in the efficiency of the stock market. The Crash just gave us a lesson on how fast this market can respond to changing conditions when it needs to. The Crash was merely a manifestation of investors *anticipating* the economic downturn that we are *only now* experiencing."

Bellow smiled broadly. "I know. I know. You've explained all that to me before. But I hadn't thought of your first point about greater volume. *Diversification!* I told you our move into brokerage would pay off in more ways than one."

Winslowe replied, "Hardly a mere *move,* Chief. With our global crossing network, we've cornered the fees on nearly all the trading done by U.S. investors and much of the trading done by foreigners throughout the world."

Smiling, Hunter added, "It's hardly *brokerage.* No more brokers. No more dealers or specialists, either. What we have is *matchmaking!* One gigantic computer network matching buyers who are willing to buy at a given price with sellers willing to sell at the same price—at a fee of no more than a penny a share to each."

Bellow was really beaming now. "The Stock Crossing and Routing Exchange (SCARE). Open 24 hours per day, 7 days per week. And with roughly 8 billion shares traded every day, those pennies add up to nearly $60 billion in annual revenue for B&H. I'd say SCARE was one hell of a great investment. Wouldn't you, Whyte?"

"Obviously—by the way, volume has been running at nearly *10 billion* shares lately. But, before we start feeling guilty over our good fortune, remember that SCARE doesn't benefit just us. Because the only stocks that sell through NASDAQ dealers now are the *smallest* companies, SCARE has reduced the cost of trading *in general.* And because anticipated trading costs are incorporated into stockholders' expected return requirements, SCARE has undoubtedly resulted in a reduction in the cost of equity capital for firms through out the world. *That* means a *stimulus* to investment spending."

"Hmm. . . . You mean to say then that B&H is doing its best to prop up the level of capital spending. *We're doing our best to soften this recession!*"

"Exactly."

Changing gears, Bellow turned to his president. "Logan, have we sent that check to the Republican candidate yet?"

"Went out in today's mail, Chief. But speaking of bad news for the firm, aren't we forgetting Bill Wilder, the independent."

Bellow: "Bill Wilder? What an idiot! Wants to impose more regulations on the financial markets, and I hear he's starting to focus on SCARE in particular, as if we don't have to contend with enough rules now. The man's a mental case! They say he's got a Ph.D. in finance, yet! Must be an *honorary* degree. He sure doesn't know anything about *real* finance."

Frowning in response to Bellow's comment, Hunter became more serious. "Let's just say he sure doesn't seem to know much about *Modern* Finance. Anyone with a *first class* MBA knows that capital markets are efficient. As I've explained to you many times before, Brighton, at any given moment in time, the price of a stock always accurately reflects the best information available about the underlying worth of the company. Given that the stock market prices fairly and efficiently, regulations can only get in the way. And they'll get in the way of the stock market's *crucial* mission in the capital economy. By setting relative stock prices, the market sets the relative cost of acquiring capital for different companies. Suppose, for example, that consumers decide that they want more of a certain product. They'll start buying it, driving up its price and the profits of the firm that's manufacturing it. If the firm is to expand production to satisfy consumer demand, it must acquire capital. If it is to acquire capital *at a fair price,* the stock market must respond to the firm's higher profitability by driving the price of its stock up to an appropriate level. Regulations just interfere with this process. If the company doesn't get the capital to expand its productive capacity, consumers don't get more of what they want."

Bellow was becoming increasingly irritated. "Well, regulations may interfere with the efficiency of the capital market, but I'm not as concerned about *that* as I am about their impact on the welfare of this firm. With SCARE, with our underwriting functions, and with our role in facilitating mergers, takeovers and spin-offs, B&H is making vital contributions to international finance. Just as more regulations will limit the ability of other firms to acquire capital at a fair price, so they will limit our ability to earn a fair rate of return on our investments. In my opinion, Wilder's *mere existence* as a political force stands as a *threat* to all of us."

"Calm down, Chief. You've got your blood pressure up 50 points again. Happens every time you talk about that guy. Maybe we could use a drink. How about some brandy?"

"Good idea, Logan. Whyte, let's go into my office, and I'll pour you some of the best French cognac you've ever tasted."

"Can't turn that down, Brighton. Please lead the way."

Brighton Bellow, the most powerful man in America, rose and led his colleagues into his enormous office. In crossing the 100-foot expanse separating them from the bar, they approached the panorama of the Manhattan skyline and what remained of the setting sun. They were able to view most of the city from an unbelievable one-way window that stretched 30 feet from floor to ceiling and 100 feet from end to end.

Logan filled the bottoms of three large snifters, and the three men took in the view.

Bellow broke the silence, as he raised his glass for a toast. "Here's to the perks associated with power and success. Gentlemen, as you know, we stand here looking through the largest single pane of glass in the world. It's six times larger than any other window in the building and nearly three times as large as any in the world. It took two Sikorsky helicopters and $30 million to get it up here. But it was worth it. Don't you think?"

Certain that the view would someday soon be his, Winslowe replied, "Sure was, Chief. Frankly, I've never seen a view to compare with this in all Manhattan."

Bellow swirled the liquid in his glass and turned to Winslowe. "Logan, tell me something. Does this Wilder creep really have a ghost of a chance in this election?"

"Not really, Chief. The American public doesn't want more regulations any more than we do. Besides, he's the former director of the IRS. Who's going to want someone like that as their president?"

Hunter smiled knowingly as he sipped his brandy. "Mmmm. Good stuff, Brighton. By the way, Logan, you did see that he was up *five* points in the last poll taken *after* the Democratic convention. *Somebody* seems to be taking the man seriously."

Brighton Bellow's eyes narrowed as he considered Hunter's remark. Then he turned to his president.

"Logan, listen carefully. I want to keep in touch with Wilder's campaign at all times. I want our best external security executive on the job—effective immediately."

"You've got it, Chief. I'll put Truman on it first thing in the morning."

"Put him on it *tonight,* Logan. Put him on it *right now.*"

As Logan Winslowe spoke to his wrist-phone, Bellow's eyes fixed on the setting sun.

Although Brighton Bellow didn't know it, the sun marked the very spot in New Jersey where, 100 miles to the west, the campaign of Bill Wilder was speeding directly at them, on board a train called the Eastern Express.

THE EASTERN EXPRESS

"Single malt please."

"Which one would you like, Ms. Meyer?"

"I'll have the Glen Morangie Port Wood Finish."

"Sure thing."

Tiffany Meyer watched Gary, the bartender, reach below the bar for the bottle of Scotch. He poured her drink and placed it on the bar.

Tiffany took it and turned. To her dismay, she found herself face to face with Dan Ronaldson, a veteran reporter who had been assigned to cover this leg of Wilder's campaign. Ronaldson had been on her back for most of the day, and he wasn't looking for news.

"Hi Dollface! Can I buy you a drink?"

Tiffany's emerald-green eyes pierced deeply into his brain. "So tell me, what's the matter with *you?*"

Ronaldson's eyes brightened. He was finally getting a response. "Whadiya mean *me?*"

"I mean, most *flies* would be smart enough to know I've already got a drink in my hand, and they also *buzz off* properly when shooed. So. . . . What's the matter with *you?*"

"Listen, forget it, lady."

"Don't worry Ronaldson; you're *easy* to forget. *Real* easy."

Tiffany brushed him aside and made her way to the circular stairway leading up to the observation deck. As she rounded the stairs at the top, her eyes caught the last of the sun setting toward the rear of the train, over the New Jersey skyline. The windows of the observation car went nearly from the floor to the very top of the ceiling.

Renting this car on the Eastern Express had been her idea, and a good one at that. It had carried the campaign from Chicago to Indianapolis to Cincinnati and now finally to New York. The best part was that, in addition to her staff, there was enough room on the car for a fairly large contingent of reporters, most of whom, unlike Ronaldson, were interested in a story. Happily, her candidate is quickly becoming a story that interests a lot of people.

Unlike the Republicans, he had a plan for dealing with the economy, and unlike the Democrats, his plan didn't call for a massive tax increase.

Wilder has had his sights on a political career for some time. He moved to the Internal Revenue Service in 1982, leaving a tenured position as Bainebright Distinguished Professor of Finance at the University of Michigan. The ambitious and hard-working Wilder had worked his way to the top of the IRS ranks like a prairie fire in a drought and had been appointed director in 1986. Tiffany Meyer had served as his chief counsel for the last 18 months. During this time, tight bonds of respect and friendship had formed between them. Wilder had an inventive and creative mind. Meyer was extremely quick, street smart, and knew the law inside and out; what's more, she was a natural leader. To know her was to respect and admire her—simple as that.

The dynamic duo knew what they had, and what they had to do. Wilder resigned his position as director of the IRS; Tiffany took a 1-year leave of absence. They then began raising funds for their campaign.

It was rough going at first. But they soon found their logical target—voters who were appalled at the thought of writing bigger checks to the IRS and now were afraid that a tax increase would make a rather frightening economic situation even worse.

In a matter of 6 months, they had a war chest large enough to launch their fledgling campaign in style. Wilder began the campaign as a Republican, but after finishing well down in the pack in the first four primaries, he dropped from the field to continue as an Independent. From that point on, it was a matter of talking up their program. Point and counterpoint. Talk show after talk show.

Now, 5 months later, all their work seemed to be paying off. Wilder was actually being mentioned in the polls, drawing 10% of voter support. His campaign was news. And that was all this duo needed to break away.

Looking down the length of the observation car, Tiffany saw the lights of the city begin to illuminate the darkness of the eastern sky. Grand Central Station was no more than 60 minutes away.

At the end of the car, Bill Wilder was engaged in conversation with a dark-haired man about 30 years of age. Tiffany walked the length of the car to join them.

"Hi, Bill. How about an introduction?"

"Tiffany, I'd like you to meet Tim Harrington. Tim's a feature writer for the *Wall Street Journal.* Tim, I'd like you to meet Tiffany Meyer, my campaign manager."

Tiffany, it's a pleasure to meet you. I've been hearing good things about the way you're running Bill's campaign. You guys are beginning to make a splash. Tell me the secret of your success."

"Simple, Tim. We've got a good man here and an economic plan that appeals to a lot of people. What else do you need to be president?"

"Tiffany, that overqualifies him these days. Bill, why don't you run your proposals for dealing with the economy by me right now?"

"If you guys don't mind, I think I'll sit in on this." Tiffany took the seat next to Wilder, directly across from the *Journal* reporter. As Wilder prepared to begin his pitch, Tiffany surveyed her candidate.

As usual, Bill's blond hair, graying at the temples, was perfectly in place. Wilder carried his 55 years well—looked about 49. His winning smile was particularly engaging. Tiffany had always found him attractive as a man, but their relationship had never completed the journey from colleagues to friends to lovers. Perhaps some day. . . . The thought of becoming First Lady crossed Tiffany's mind . . . forget it!

Wilder began the pitch. "At this stage of the race, without question, the number one concern of the American people is the deteriorating economy.

There are three candidates in the race. The first is a member of my own Republican Party. I fully respect his credentials, but he's got no plan other than business as usual. If this were a normal recession, that might even be acceptable, but this doesn't appear to be a normal recession. Things are beginning to get worse *fast,* and that calls for decisive action on the part of those who expect to lead the American people. The Democrat has a plan, but by my assessment, it's a bad one. He sees the ultimate source of our economic problems as the federal budget deficit. He wants to eliminate, or at least reduce, the deficit by raising taxes."

Harrington interrupted, "Don't you think the deficit is a real problem, Bill?"

"Look. I'm not trying to minimize the problems we've got with the deficit and the national debt. These are important *long-run* problems that we've ultimately got to come to grips with. But *now* is not the time for a *full frontal assault* on these problems. This economy is badly in need of a *fix.* Taking money away from consumers by raising their taxes to pay off the deficit will have a *depressing* effect on the economy. In my book, that's 10 times worse than the Republican's plan of holding a pat hand. At least their hand is neutral. At least it's not *detrimental!*"

"Yeah. I have to agree with you. This is a real tough cookie. What we really need is a tax cut, but with the deficit, we've got our backs to the wall on that one."

"You're right. Our hands are pretty much tied in terms of getting out of this recession with an aggressive fiscal policy. Worse yet, the Federal Reserve's got its pedal to the metal, but it doesn't seem to be helping very much. You can only go so far in trying to expand real growth with monetary policy before you light the fires of inflation, and all the stock market needs right now is an unexpected bout of inflation."

"And that brings us to your program, Bill. You seem to want to attack the problem through the stock market. I have to admit—at a minimum, it's a novel approach!"

"To say that we've got problems with the stock market is an understatement. You guys have been running front-page news about the market in just about every edition of the *WSJ.* Up. Down. Rally. Collapse. Correction. Reversal. Nobody seems to be able to figure out what in the hell is going on."

"True enough. I've never seen volatility like this before."

"An it's scaring the *hell* out of people. They don't know what to make of it. Between the volatility and the Great Crash and the losses since the Great Crash, they're keeping their wallets in their back pockets. Consumer confidence is down. *Way down.*"

"And you want to do something about the stock market."

"Look. Between the introduction of trading through SCARE and the closing of the New York Stock Exchange 2 years ago, it's no longer business as usual on Wall Street. In light of the major changes in market conditions, I think we've got to take stock of what we're dealing with. We've got to take a long, hard look at the situation, separate the good from the bad, and set up a sound program of regulations to eliminate what's bad about SCARE."

"So what's so bad about it?"

"Tim, I'm just not prepared to go into that right now. Just wouldn't be prudent. If elected, I'm promising this. My first act as president will be to establish an executive task force on financial reform. I'm also going to ask Congress to hold hearings as well. Between the two branches, we should be able to come up with a sound policy for dealing with the problems in the stock market."

"Problems in the stock market. . . . But how do we know that volatility is really a problem in the *stock market?* How do we know that the market's volatility isn't really reflecting problems in the *economy?*"

"The Great Crash came *first. Then* we had the acceleration in the economic decline."

Let me tell you something, Bill. Just last week, I interviewed Dr. Whyte Hunter, the chief economist for Badsworth and Hyde. He said there's *nothing* wrong with the stock market. He says it's the one sector of the economy where the so-called invisible hand works really well. He says the natural forces of competition force stock prices to keep in line with fair values. He says if stock prices are volatile, it's because fair values are volatile, and that's because of the current volatile nature of the economy."

Sipping the last of the scotch from her glass, Tiffany couldn't resist. "And how does the great Whyte Hunter explain the Second Great Crash? Did the invisible *fist* smash stock prices down to make them sell at 70% of what they were worth on the previous day?"

"I actually asked him that. He claims that the Crash is actually evidence of the efficient market in action. He claims that the market saw our present economic problems coming around the corner. The market saw that we were about to pay the bill for all those years of red ink!"

Tiffany again. "Come *on,* Tim! This country's been running on red ink for more than 10 years. You mean to tell us that the market finally woke up to the problem on the morning of June 6?"

"Tiffany, these aren't *my* thoughts; they're *Hunter's.* However, if he were here, I think I can guess his response."

"Which would be?"

"The Crash was an *accurate* move on the part of the market. After all, we really *are* in a stew right now, aren't we?"

"This is a chicken-or-egg type question, isn't it? Did the stock market *predict* our problems or did it *cause* them?"

"That's right. These efficient-market types seem to be able to weasel out of any potentially embarrassing situation. But you have to admit, there are plenty of eggheads like Hunter walking around, and believe me, they *all* spell trouble for you and Bill. They *all* will claim that the stock market is just fine the way it is. And that you're only going to *screw it up* with your proposed regulations."

"Is that what you believe, Tim?"

"I'm not sure what I believe. *Yet.* But I'll tell you one thing. Your campaign is going to have to contend with the likes of Whyte Hunter. You better be ready for him *and* his friends."

Wilder replied, "*Tell me about it.* Bryant Grumble is interviewing Hunter and me tomorrow night live on television!"

"Told you so. Good luck with *that* one!"

With that, Tim Harrington rose, shook hands, and proceeded to make his way through the train to his seat on the lower level.

Tiffany turned to Wilder. "We're going to need more ammunition for our case. We need a more convincing story. We need to break the chicken from the egg."

"How're we going to do that?"

"I'm not sure. . . . But listen, I've got an appointment tomorrow with a professor at Columbia University. He's supposed to have some interesting thoughts on this efficient-markets thing. Maybe *he* can help us."

"But what am I supposed to do about tomorrow night?"

"Just wing it, until I get our ammunition."

BULLETS

The elevator doors opened, and Tiffany Meyer stepped into the eighth-floor hallway of the building housing the School of Business at Columbia University. The building was surprisingly undistinguished—even nondescript—for a university as distinguished as this one. But universities are distinguished by their *faculty. Buildings* can be very misleading.

Glad to be out of an elevator that had turned out to be a rather crowded local (as opposed to an express), Tiffany turned down the hall, and headed for Room 824—Professor Mayer's office.

The top half of Mayer's office door was a window of rough translucent glass. Through the glass, and between the door and the exterior window on the other side of the room, Tiffany could make out the outline of a large object. She rapped on the door, and the object responded. It rose, circled around something, and opened the door.

Tiffany extended her hand. "Professor Mayer, my name is Tiffany Meyer. I believe we have an appointment for 4:00 o'clock."

Mayer's eyes widened. "Ms. Meyer. . . . That's right. . . . By gosh, it had almost slipped my mind. But of course. Please come in. Mind if I call you Tiffany?"

Entering. "Of course not. Let me tell you, I'm very grateful for a small piece of your time."

"Not at all. Actually *I'm* the one who's appreciative. Bill Wilder has been very much in the news of late. Frankly, I have been looking forward to meeting you."

Tiffany sat in one of two leather-on-walnut chairs in front of Professor Mayer's desk. Professor Mayer was a tall man—about 6'4". A bit paunchy, even for his middle 60s. His head was adorned with a strip of white hair that extended from the top of one ear around the back of his head to the other. His spectacles, however, rested on a rather distinguished looking nose. Under this was a full mustache, also in white. All in all, a stereotypical academic, Tiffany thought.

The left wall was lined with books. The right held photographs, many of which had likely been taken somewhere in Europe, of Mayer with friends and family. Behind the professor's desk, and in front of the window, two standard 50″ computer monitors partially blocked the view of the Chrysler Building and the Needle on the far side of Central Park.

"Let's see. . . . . Meyer. Is that German by any chance?"

"Why, yes, it is."

"Most of *my* family stems from the little country of Switzerland—a place I have to admit I'm really very fond of. I try to visit there as often as possible. How about you? Do you like to go back to *your* roots from time to time?"

"Well, although the name Meyer *is* German, my ancestors are more scattered than yours apparently are. Many are Dutch, and I do get to Amsterdam from time to time. And it *is* one of my favorite cities."

Tiffany suspected her time with the professor was limited, and she wanted to make good use of it. "Professor, I don't want to waste your valuable time. Please don't consider me rude if I get right down to business."

"Not at all. Tell me what's on your mind."

"You spoke before as though you know something about our campaign. Is that true?"

"Well, I *am* a professor of finance and your campaign is very much about finance, isn't it?"

Tiffany was pleased with his familiarity. Now to see if he was sympathetic to their position.

"Yes, it is. As you probably know, we're advocating financial reform—specifically, a series of regulatory measures focusing on SCARE, the new system for trading stocks."

"Well, the stock market's certainly been in a terrible state of late, hasn't it? We haven't seen a period of prolonged, extreme volatility like this in a long, long time. Not since the late 20s and 30s."

Tiffany interrupted. "Professor, let me be direct. I have an important question for you."

"What's that?"

"What's your position on the Efficient Markets Hypothesis?"

Mayer smiled broadly. "Well, that's one right out of the blue, coming from a presidential campaign manager!"

"It's an important issue to us. One we're going to have to contend with. And I'm very interested in hearing how you come down on it."

"Well, you couldn't exactly say I'm *neutral* on the issue. As any of my former students will tell you—I think, and I have always thought, that this notion about the efficient market is a bunch of hot air! *Just nonsense!* How people can still believe in it after experiencing the events of October the 19th and June the 6th is beyond me. To say that 20% and 30% single-day moves constitute efficient responses to new information is absolutely *crazy!* What new information? The only thing newsworthy at the time was the state of *panic* in the stock market itself."

At that moment a younger man walked past the door and then stopped. He stepped back and then poked his head into Professor Mayer's office. "Hi R.W. How are you today?"

"Just fine, Woodson, and I hope you're doing as well."

"Sure. Mind introducing me to the young lady?"

"Professor Woodson, I'd like to introduce you to Tiffany Meyer. As you may know, she's running Bill Wilder's campaign."

He shook Tiffany's hand. "Sure, I saw you last Sunday on 'Meet the Media.' You spoke of reform in the financial markets."

"That's right. Was I convincing?"

Woodson smiled knowingly. "The faculty at Columbia have great faith in the financial markets."

"You mean you believe they're efficient."

"True. Mess around with something as perfect as the stock market, and you're bound to foul things up."

Tiffany sensed that trying to convince this one of anything was pretty much a waste of time.

"Well, it's been nice meeting you, but my time is limited and, if you don't mind, I'd like to continue to pick Professor Mayer's brain."

"I'm sure you'll find that R.W.'s views concur with mine. Right, R.W.?"

"Well it *has* taken some time, but I think you guys have finally convinced me."

"We knew you'd come around."

Woodson smiled at Tiffany, paid his respects and continued down the hall.

Tiffany noticed some distress in Professor Mayer's voice.

"Tiffany, would you mind shutting the door?"

Tiffany rose from her chair and closed the door. "Professor Mayer! You just told me the notion of an efficient stock market was sheer nonsense. Now you say you agree with Professor Woodson. Just what *is* your position, anyway?"

"Listen, Tiffany. You have to be careful about what you say around here these days. Ever since they eliminated tenure 3 years ago, your position on an issue could well cost you your job—especially on *that* issue."

"And what's so special about *that* issue?"

"Just about all the finance professors in this school were trained in an economics department. They don't have the faintest idea about how to go about investing money. They can't train students! So they preach market efficiency. In an efficient market, training isn't necessary. A monkey can be expected to do as well as a highly trained analyst."

"Woodson is a member of what we call the Efficient Markets Police. He sits on the research and curriculum committee. They monitor the research we do and what we teach in the classroom."

"You mean you can't teach what you believe?"

"I teach the Efficient Markets Hypothesis. And my students read from a text called *Efficient Investing,* authored by Woodson himself."

"How demeaning. Why?"

"I've got 3 years left to retirement. Tenure is history. It's the only way I can keep my job."

Tiffany shook her head in disbelief. "Professor Mayer, please know that everything you say to me today will be held in strictest confidence. Please tell me what you really believe!"

Tiffany held him with her eyes. "Do you believe that the Second Great Crash was an anticipation of the current downturn in the economy?"

Professor Mayer paused for a moment and then continued the discussion interrupted by Woodson. "Not for a minute. There wasn't a shred of evidence at the time that things were going to get this bad."

"And what about the volatility since then? Not an efficient and rational reflection of the uncertain state of present economic conditions?"

"No way! What we've really got is a market that has *scared* the daylights out of *itself.* Afraid of what it might do next. And listen. The volatility was on the high side *before* the Crash. It's been high ever since trading was taken over by that crossing network."

Tiffany's eyes widened. "SCARE? You actually think there may be a connection between SCARE and the volatility?"

"I do. But it's going to take a while to explain my position."

Mayer began: "In my opinion, stock volatility has two components. I call the first *fundamental volatility.* This is the day-to-day or minute-to-minute variability in the movement in stock prices that is caused by the arrival of new information and its impact on fair or intrinsic values. This part of the volatility is related to changing economic conditions and changes related to the character of the firms behind the stocks—the nature of their lines of business, the way they produce their products, and the structure of the financial claims on their assets. If the market *were* really efficient, fundamental volatility would be the whole story. It would be the *only* source of risk in the equity market. *But the market is not efficient.* It makes mistakes. Prices *do* deviate from their intrinsic values. And the deviations occur in *varying* degrees. The time-varying pricing errors made by the *inefficient* market are the source of a second component of volatility— *technical volatility.* Few people would argue with this, *in concept.* The *real* argument is over the relative size of the two components. I, for one, believe that the technical component actually *dominates* in size. I also believe it's *unstable.*"

"Unstable? What do you mean?"

The professor rotated his chair to face his computer keyboard, located between the two monitors. He clicked his mouse until an odd-looking graph appeared on the left screen. It reminded Tiffany of the chart produced by a seismograph during an earthquake—only this one ran sideways rather than up and down.

Professor Mayer began to explain. "On this graph we're plotting time, in trading days, on the horizontal axis and the day-to-day *percentage change* in the value of the S&P 500 stock index on the vertical axis. When you're above the horizontal line, the daily return to the index is positive; when you're below, it's negative. Now, it may look as though there are as many down days as up, but if you accumulated these daily changes, you would see that the value of the index itself has a nice positive trend to it. . . . But, getting back to my point, look at the varying amplitude of movement up and down in the daily rate of return over the last 5 years. See how, in some periods, the market's return volatility becomes suddenly much bigger ("Like in an earthquake!" thought Tiffany), and then it slowly declines back to normal levels. And look how *often* this happens. Volatility shifts are a *common* event. Why, it's not uncommon for volatility to shift several times in a single year. Tiffany, it is simply the case that these shifts are much *too* common and much *too* large to be caused by changes in the character of companies or the nature of economic conditions."

"Then we must be seeing shifts in the technical volatility, right?"

"*Yes,* Tiffany. I think you're exactly right. I think we're looking at changes in the variability in the magnitudes of the pricing errors being made by the market. Fundamental volatility is undoubtedly *contained* in this picture. But I think it's technical volatility that accounts for the dominant features in the graphic. It's the technical volatility that is changing repeatedly over time."

Tiffany's attention drifted toward the *end* of the graph. It looked like "The Big One" they were waiting for in California—the Big One followed by a prolonged series of after-shocks. Following the major "quake," it looked like volatility remained 3 or 4 times as big as it had been before.

Tiffany pointed to the screen. "What's that big burst near the end? Is *that* the Great Crash?"

"Sure is. I'm not sure if you can make this out, but note that in the period *prior* to the Second Great Crash, volatility was at a relatively high level. And I don't think it's coincidental that the rise in volatility was coincident with trading activity predominantly moving to SCARE."

Tiffany tried to press the professor on his suspicions relating SCARE to market volatility. "Tell me, Professor, does volatility always behave like this during a market melt-down?"

A few clicks of the mouse sent the *right* monitor into action. "As you probably know, for some time now, call options have been written on the S&P 500 stock index. These options give you the right to "buy" the index at a stated *exercise price* at any time before they expire. By far the most important determinant of the market value of these options is the volatility of the index itself. The more volatile the index, the larger the chance that the index will rise above the exercise price, making the options valuable to their owners. Traders use sophisticated models to price these options. To use these models, you enter your estimate of S&P volatility into the model, along with the option's characteristics (expiration date, exercise price, etc.), and the model tells you how much the option is worth, based on your estimate of the volatility. You can also run this process *backward*. Rather than entering the volatility, you can enter the option's current market price and the model will tell you how big the volatility must be to justify the price. Since the market sets the price, the models are, therefore, telling you what the market thinks about its own volatility."

A new graph appeared on the *right* screen [see Figure 2.1]. Once again, time in trading days was plotted on the horizontal axis. In this graph, the time period covered was 1986 to 1990. The vertical axis was labeled "Implied Standard

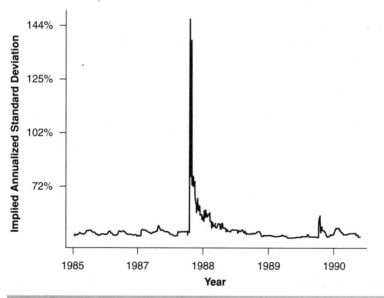

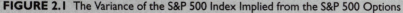

FIGURE 2.1 The Variance of the S&P 500 Index Implied from the S&P 500 Options

Implied variance is a weighted average of the implied volatilities of the closest-to-expiration at-the-money put and call options on the S&P 500 Index with dividend adjustments.

Source: Adapted from Naifu, Cuny, and Haugen, "Stock Volatility and the Levels of the Basis and Open Interest in Future Contracts," *Journal of Finance,* March 1995, p. 288.

Deviation." A line showing the time-series of implied volatility moved across the graph, hovering close to zero until the latter part of 1987. Then, seemingly on a single day, it spiked *like a rocket* to nearly 150! Then, over the next few months, it gradually fell to a more normal level.

Professor Mayer began. "On this graph, we're plotting the annualized implied volatility, consistent with the daily prices of S&P 500 options. It's easy to pick out the '87 crash, isn't it? I'd like some efficient-market fanatic to try to explain how fundamental volatility managed to increase by 7 times in a single day, October the 19th, when nothing of any great economic significance happened on that day. That day was historic *only* in terms of what happened to the market itself. What you're seeing here is an explosion in *technical,* not *fundamental* volatility. And this graph clearly shows just how *large* and how *unstable* technical volatility really is!"

Tiffany could hardly believe what she was seeing. "That is, quite simply, incredible! How does something like that happen?"

"That's a very good question. Here's my answer. . . . Suppose *you* were the market. How would you learn about the magnitudes of your two components of volatility? You could learn about your *fundamental* volatility by analyzing the character of the companies behind the stocks as well as economic conditions and the prevailing level of economic uncertainty. But what about your *technical* volatility? How are you going to learn about *that?*"

"I know I'm supposed to be the market, but I still don't know the answer to your question. Enlighten me."

"By watching *yourself.* By watching *your own* behavior, you *learn* about your technical volatility. You learn about how emotional or sloppy you are at the moment in your pricing of stocks. By observing what you are doing *in the present,* you learn about what you are capable of doing *in the future.*"

Professor Mayer continued: "Many years ago, in his presidential address to the American Finance Association, Mark Rubinstein took the concept of implied volatility to a second stage. You see, there are actually many different options on the S&P index. Some have different expiration dates. Others have different exercise prices. By examining the relative prices of S&P options with different exercise prices, Rubinstein figured out a way of determining the market's estimate of the probabilities of seeing various values for the index in the future, when the options expire."

Several more clicks resulted in a new graph on the left screen [see Figure 2.2]. "Rubinstein calculated this distribution of probabilities for the S&P 500 index value some 164 days into the future. That is, at 11:00 A.M. on January 2,

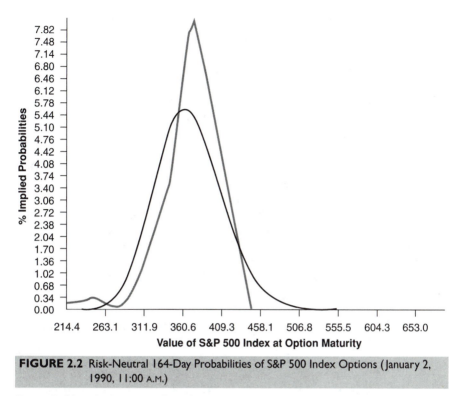

FIGURE 2.2 Risk-Neutral 164-Day Probabilities of S&P 500 Index Options (January 2, 1990, 11:00 A.M.)

Source: Rubinstein, Mark, "Implied Binomial Trees," *Journal of Finance,* July 1994, p. 784.

1990, the market thought that these were the probabilities for different values for the index 164 days into the future. The other, darker distribution is a normal distribution with the same mean and variance."

Tiffany thought the probability distribution looked reasonable enough, except for the "bump" in the left tail. What was that? Mayer anticipated her thoughts. "Look at the left tail. In his address, Rubinstein called this 'market crash-o-phobia.' Note the relatively high probabilities in the tail for a market decline of about 35%. At least, as of 1990, the market had it in its mind that another crash was a distinct possibility. Bumps like these were not present in the distributions calculated from prices established *before* October the 19th. But they appear *afterward,* because the market had *learned* that events like the 19th *were distinctly possible.*"

"Now look at the right graph, showing implied volatility around the '87 Crash. See the smaller spike toward the latter part of 1989? This was the event of October the 13th. It was set off by the collapse of the UAL merger. The entire market fell nearly 20% in less than an hour. I believe that a move of this speed and force was made possible only because the market had *learned* what it was capable of doing, 2 years before on the 19th."

"Tiffany, the market watches itself and it *learns* about its nature. To see this, consider the events that led us to the Crash on October 19, 1987. Nothing extraordinary was happening *outside* of the market. The really interesting things were happening *inside.* The first significant event happened on October the 6th. On that day, stock prices fell by about 3%. Again, imagine that you're the market, watching your own behavior. You've got a prior opinion about the magnitude of your technical volatility—a concept of the probability distribution of your daily rates of return. And you've set stock prices at a level to produce an expected return that's consistent with your concept of the volatility. That 3% return you've just experienced would have to have come from deep into the left-hand tail of your prior distribution. But that's okay. Events like that will happen every so often, even if your prior estimate of the volatility is correct."

"Now we enter the week before the crash. On three of the first four days of the week, we have events similar in magnitude to the event of the sixth. Although it's difficult to see because of the scale of the implied volatility graph on the right, the prices of S&P 500 options were already changing to reflect the market's inflating estimate of its technical volatility."

"Then we hit the Friday before what has now come to be known as "Black Monday." With estimates of volatility up, investors want a higher expected return to compensate them for investing in the more volatile market. Higher future returns are possible only if the current level of prices is more heavily discounted. On Friday, the market suffered the biggest dollar price decline in its history. The probability that this kind of price behavior is consistent with even the revised estimates of volatility is remote. Estimates of technical volatility are dramatically revised *again,* calling for an even bigger price adjustment at the opening bell on Monday. The decline at the open on Monday twice the dollar magnitude of the historic decline on Friday. We get another dramatic revision in the volatility estimate, followed by another price decline, and down we go, until trading comes to a grinding halt because the specialists are no longer willing to make a market in the presence of this kind of panicked insanity."

The professor paused for a moment, pondering a thought. "Stock markets are populated by people. Stock prices change in response to the orders of people. It shouldn't surprise us that panics in the stock market follow patterns similar to panic attacks in individuals."

"How so?"

"Some time ago, a psychologist named David Clark suggested a sequence of events that might induce a panic attack.[1] Clark believes that a stimulus (coming from within the body or from the external environment) is perceived by an individual as a threat. The person becomes apprehensive and hypervigilant, repeatedly scanning the body for other sensations. This internal focus allows the individual to notice sensations that most other people would not be aware of. Once noticed, these sensations are taken as further evidence of serious disorder. This now becomes the perceived threat, which continues the downward spiral. The crucial event in the sequence, however, is a misinterpretation of bodily sensations, and these sensations are most commonly the result of a preceding anxiety."

Tiffany was fascinated. "That's actually *scary*. Market melt-downs seemingly coming from *nowhere*. From *within* the market itself!"

Tiffany pondered the thought for a moment. Then she expressed a doubt. "But, Professor, wouldn't investors realize that a sequence of unlucky, bad market days is entirely consistent with the previous distribution of stock returns? I mean, if you wait long enough—experience a sufficient number of trades and price changes—highly unusual sequences of price changes *will* happen. Won't rational investors take this element of pure chance into account? Why would a few bad days call for a complete revision in the notion of what the probability distribution of returns looks like?"

"You're absolutely correct, Tiffany. If investors behaved perfectly *rationally,* and if the *fundamental* volatility of stock returns remained constant, opinions wouldn't turn so quickly on the basis of recent experience. But suppose stock prices *aren't* based on rational investor behavior. Consider this. Two behavioral researchers named Kahneman and Tversky have shown, convincingly in my opinion, that, in establishing their beliefs, individuals tend to *overweight* more recent information and *underweight* information established over the long run. Given that this propensity actually describes investor behavior, then my theory that a sequence of extreme events may first create a revision in expectations, which then calls for a market response that then reinforces the sequence, creating further revisions and a possible price spiral, follows logically."

"Seems logical to me. But, Professor, you seemed to indicate before that you saw a connection between SCARE and the current high level of market volatility. What is it?"

"Well, if my theory is correct, then it's simply a matter of experiencing a sufficient number of trades and observed price changes until the market encounters a sequence of extremes sufficient to trigger a sufficient revision in its expectations to produce a burst in technical volatility. SCARE has done three things to significantly increase the probability of experiencing these events. *First,* the introduction of SCARE has increased the number of weekly trading hours from 32½ to 168—24 hours per day, 7 days per week. *Second,* by reducing trading costs, it has dramatically increased the number of trades experienced in a given unit of time. And the more trades we experience, the greater the probability of hitting the required sequence. *Finally,* SCARE has shoved the market and its volatility directly in the face of every investor in America. By simply clicking on their mice, they can see what's happening at any given moment—24 hours a day."

To demonstrate his point, the professor pulled the market up on his left screen. A graph of the current value of the S&P 500 stock index appeared—moving, with alarming volatility—in *real* time.

"Professor, besides the fact that it is currently scaring the hell out of people, can this volatility thing be a source of serious concern? Can it do any real damage?"

"Definitely. It can act as a real impediment to consumption and capital investment spending by business firms."

"How so?"

"In three ways. First, if you happen to be one of those who believe that the market is relatively efficient, than you must also believe that an increased level of market volatility is a *reflection* of an increase in fundamental uncertainty about the future state of the economy. This may lead chief financial officers, who were trained in business schools and happen to take stock market behavior seriously, to view the prospects for capital investments in a more pessimistic light. If *technical* volatility is mistakenly viewed as *fundamental,* than we have a serious concern. Rather than being a mere *reflection* of the economic problem, volatility in the market potentially becomes a *source of the underlying problem.*"

"Second, an increase in technical volatility may cause managers to raise their *minimum return requirements* for capital investments."

"You see, scared investors require high expected rates of return to compensate them for the risk they think they're going to be experiencing in the future. Right now, the volatility is roughly six times what it was before the Great Crash. Under reasonable behavioral assumptions, this implies that the required risk premium on stocks is roughly 36 times bigger than it was. If it was 6% before, it may be 210% now. And that 210% *can* be a *huge* part of the cost of capital for U.S. industry."

"What do you mean *can* be?"

"Everything depends on how *long* the volatility is expected to persist. Investors will require the additional premium return only for as long as they expect to experience the additional volatility. If it's only for a few months, as it was in 1987, the burst will have only a negligible impact on the long-run cost of capital. But if volatility persists, as it did after the 1929 crash, investors may *project* its continuance for a prolonged period into the future. And the longer it sticks around, the more prolonged this projected period may be."

The professor continued. "I think this actually happened in 1929. Stock market volatility became a *long-term problem.* There were several contributing factors that compounded into the economic debacle that has become known as the Great Depression. For example, the downturn in real output actually began in August of 1929, but it accelerated dramatically following the October calamity in the stock market. Tight money is well accepted as the explanation for the severe collapse in industrial production that occurred in 1931, *but 1930 is the real mystery.* The fact that short-term interest rates fell dramatically after 1929 supports the notion that nonmonetary forces were transforming a mild recession into something far more serious.[2] Seasonally adjusted industrial production declined by less than 2% between August and October 1929, *but it declined by 24% in 1930."*

"What was the catalyst behind the downturn? I think it was the *stock market.* Now, I know that many economists dismiss that idea because they discount the magnitude of a possible impact of declining stock prices on *wealth* and, through wealth, on *consumption.* But I don't think the impact came through wealth. I think it came through the impact of stock market behavior on *uncertainty.* In my view, the falling and highly volatile stock market cast a pall of uncertainty across the entire economy."

"The uncertainty creates yet a third link between the stock market and economic conditions. I believe uncertainty affected the behavior of consumers. Suppose you are thinking of buying a car. How expensive a car should you buy? That depends on how well the car will fit into your budget in the future. An increase in uncertainty about your future income increases the probability that you will buy the wrong car now (too cheap or too expensive). An increase in uncertainty increases the value of the option to buy later when your income situation is more stable. Believe me, Tiffany, in the months following the great crash of 1929, the impact of the stock market on business conditions was very much on people's minds. And the production of consumer durable goods fell by more than 32% in 1930."

"You know, there was a study published in the prestigious *Quarterly Journal of Economics* by a Berkeley professor named Christina Romer,[3] who estimated the relationship between spending on durable goods and stock market volatility over roughly the 4 decades that preceded the 1929 crash. Romer found that, given the increase in stock volatility that occurred in 1929, her model predicted a fall of 44% in consumer durable spending versus the 32% that actually occurred."

"But remember the stock market's effect on business firms, which may be even more important. It affected (a) managerial sentiment relating to the prospects for the profitability of investment projects and (b) the return requirements for these projects, or the cost of capital. Through the impact of both, I believe that market volatility significantly reduced *capital investment*. Gross private investment actually fell by 35% in 1930. By the time we hit 1932, capital spending had all but evaporated. I believe the effects of stock market volatility on both investment and consumption turned a recession into a *depression*."

"But, Professor, I thought you said that interest rates were unusually low during the early 1930s? Why couldn't firms finance by selling bonds?"

"I'm not talking about the base, or risk-free, rate. I'm talking about the *risk premium on equities*. Remember, with the stock market in the process of collapsing, the equity buffer of U.S. industry was collapsing with it. Firms were understandably less than willing and able to put themselves in an even more precarious position by issuing more debt to finance their investments."

Professor Mayer turned once again to his mouse. A new "seismograph" replaced the contemporary market on the left screen [see Figure 2.3]. Again, the daily rate of return was being plotted against time—this time over the years 1926 through 1933. This time it looked like the quake from hell—the "Big One" *that never quieted down*.

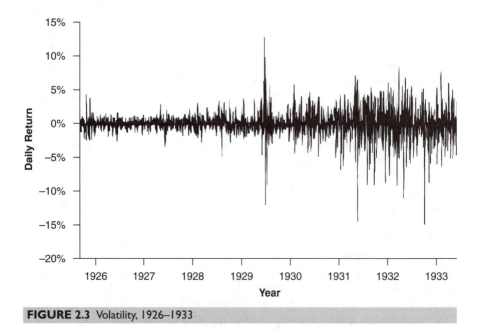

FIGURE 2.3 Volatility, 1926–1933

"In 1929, we didn't have options, so we can't plot an implied volatility series like we did for 1987 on the left screen. But you can easily get the picture in any case."

Tiffany quietly stated the obvious. "The volatility didn't go away."

"That's right. After quieting down a bit in the early part of 1930, it exploded again in June, and then it remained high during most of the 1930s."

"But weren't we well into the Great Depression by June? Wouldn't the June burst be related to a rise in *fundamental* volatility stemming from the deplorable state of the economy?"

"I don't think so. The economy began losing steam toward the end of 1929, but the downturn was widely expected to persist for only a few months. In her article, Romer presents the forecasts and analysis of forecasters like *Business Week* and *Moody's Investor Service.* Those forecasters who were less confident indicated that their uncertainty was related to the stock market crash. Even in June, most attention and concern was focused on the behavior of the *stock* market. Concerns were expressed about the economy, but only as a *potential explanation for what was going on in the stock market.* The issue was why the market was reacting so violently to the economic slowdown. An efficient-markets person might argue that investors were somehow able to foresee the oncoming debacle, but I don't see how this could be true. *The Great Depression* could hardly be anticipated based on the numbers available in October 1929. Slowdowns of the type experienced in the second half of 1929 are typically regarded by financial markets as *good* news rather than *bad.* I don't think the market was reacting to the state of the economy at all. Rather, I think the market was, once again, in the process of *scaring itself to death!*

"Just as consumers have an option to spend now or wait, the managers of business firms also have options to finance and invest now or wait. Stock market volatility created uncertainty in the minds of consumers. *And in the minds of managers.* Should they invest now or wait? Uncertainty increased the value of the option of waiting to *invest.* It also increased the value of the option associated with waiting to *finance.*

"1930, Tiffany. What happened in 1930? What does an efficient-markets person make of 1930? What does the fight over efficient markets mean? What is its importance? 1930 was a defining year in history. It's *crucial* that we come to an understanding of what was happening. *It must never happen again!*

"What happened in 1930 to set the stage for the economic debacle to come? What was going completely haywire? There was an increasing sense of fear that something was very wrong. But what was the source of that fear?

"I think it was the stock market.

"Here. Let me show you what I mean." The professor turned to his keyboard and began typing. The right screen first displayed the title, "News Archives," and then the familiar image of the front page of the *Wall Street Journal* appeared. "This is a feature article published on November 10, 1930, by a *Journal* writer named Thomas Woodlock. As you will see, Woodlock was not a believer in market efficiency."

Mayer pointed to a paragraph in the article. It read:

The condition of the stock markets today may not inaccurately be described *in general* as a "state of nerves." It is the natural penalty of the mood to which people enthusiastically yielded themselves 18 months ago. . . . The mood of 18 months ago, as we can all now see, was unreasonable in *toto*. Presently, we shall see with equal clearness on looking back that the present mood was equally unreasonable.

"As you can see, even as late as November, the *Journal* writer perceived that the state of the market was inconsistent with the state of economic conditions."

Pointing to a paragraph later in the article: "Look here. Woodlock clearly points to the market as a *source* rather than a mere *symptom* of more general economic problems."

"Nerves" are not confined to stock market circles. They are a contagious disease that tends to spread with rapidity and virulence to all circles of human activity. That the present mood of "Wall Street"—the phrase is used to specify the circles directly interested in the stock market—is infecting business in general, at least to some extent, is evident, and it is evident that infection is spreading. More than one letter has been received by the *Wall Street Journal* urging either that dealings in stocks be suspended altogether or that quotations not be published! From this may be gleaned some idea of the riot of unreason that is loose in men's minds these days.

"Tiffany, simply consider the *proximity in time* as well as the *relative significance* of both the 1929 stock market crash and the Great Depression. If you believe in efficient markets, you have no problem explaining both. An efficient-markets theorist might contend that even in October of 1929, before any numbers registering an economic downturn had been reported, the omniscient stock market was somehow able to anticipate the nature of the eminent economic debacle. But what if the market isn't omniscient at all? How to explain the proximity then? Two economic events with the word "Great" in front of their names. Why so close? By *chance*? Or by *cause, but cause coming from the reverse direction*? If the oncoming depression didn't cause the stock market crash, then *was it the crash that planted the seeds that ultimately grew into the Great Depression?*"

Professor Mayer continued, "Now, I know that a burst in technical volatility can't last indefinitely. It is likely the case that, as time went on, and as business firms increasingly cut back on their capital spending, we moved, beyond 1930, into the Great Depression. I think it's quite possible that as economic conditions deteriorated at an unprecedented rate, we may *then* have experienced a substantial increase in *fundamental* volatility. And the high level of fundamental volatility persisted through most of the decade."

"And what about today? What does the situation look like *now?*"

"I'm afraid things look more like 1929 than 1987, Tiffany." Another click brought up the current implied volatility picture in the left screen. In comparing the right with the left, Tiffany saw a clear difference. As with October 19, there was a spike on June 6, but although volatility had dropped somewhat from the stratospheric levels of the 6th, it was definitely not dissipating, as it had after the 19th."

"God! You mean we may be actually heading for a repeat of the *Great Depression?*"

"Time will tell. But I *do* think we're about to see a real test of the economic 'safety net' that was put into place during the Depression—things like deposit and unemployment insurance and such."

"Professor, I'm sitting here actually stunned! Stunned! But I need to know the policy implications of all this. What should we do? What *can* we do?"

"The solution is actually pretty direct and simple. Take steps to reduce the probability of experiencing volatility bursts. Reduce the probability of experiencing the sequence of returns that can set off a price spiral."

"How?"

"Set time limits on the trading day. *This move to 24-hour trading was a big mistake!*

"A dramatic burst in technical volatility can result in an economic downturn. But, given its size relative to fundamental volatility, the continuous presence of technical volatility bloats the risk premium in the cost of equity capital and acts as a serious and continuous drag on investment and the economy. Over the years, the compounded effects of this drag make a *tremendous difference.*

"We shouldn't be lengthening the trading day. We should be shortening it dramatically!"

WHAT'S THIS TRUMAN LOOMIN'?

Exiting the taxicab, Tiffany quickly entered the building housing NBC studios.

She had just come from the Columbia University library, where she had spent the last 2 hours checking out several aspects of Professor Mayer's story. The library's archives had provided her with access to microfilm of editions of the *Wall Street Journal* dating back to 1929. She found a perusal through these old editions to be very illuminating. She had concentrated her efforts on the paper's September, October, and December editions.

As Mayer had led her to expect, there was little or nothing negative in the way of news regarding the economy, the profitability of, or the outlook for the firms priced in the stock market. Instead, the market and its *volatility* dominated the news. The market's jitters seemed to begin following a luncheon speech by a fellow named Roger Babson. In the speech, Babson predicted a crash in the market and a downturn in business conditions. But, as far as she could tell, there was little evidence that such a downturn was in the works, at least based on the stories in the *Journal*. Instead, the paper reported almost daily on the market's volatility, beginning in the latter part of September and continuing throughout the rest of the year. Stories carrying banners like "Market Strongly Rallies" and "Market Breaks Again." Articles written about other economic and business matters were actually quite *positive*.

Then, in the middle of October, the bottom caved in.

Tiffany couldn't help but smile as she thought of it. "To think that the seeds of the Great Depression, and all that followed because of it, may have been planted by a luncheon speech."

She walked into the studio from which "Deadline Tonight," NBC's news-magazine show, was broadcast. The broadcast appeared to be over, but she saw Bill Wilder standing at the side of a desk in front of a camera. She walked over to him."

"How was the debate, Bill?"

"Well, let's just say I didn't win hands down. But the best I had hoped for against Hunter was a draw. What did you come up with at Columbia?"

"I can't wait to tell you. Let's go have dinner and I'll fill you in."

"Sounds good to me, but how'd you like to meet Bryant Grumble first?"

"Love to. Is he still here?"

Wilder looked across the studio and saw Bryant Grumble talking to two men. One was Whyte Hunter. The other was a man he didn't know. The stranger was a man of enormous stature.

Tiffany followed Wilder to the other side of the studio. As they approached the three men, she was amazed by the size of one of Grumble's companions. He was at least 6'9", and he must have tipped the scale at 300 pounds. The other man looked like he had just stepped from a Scott Fitzgerald novel. Medium height. Slightly built. Dark blue, double-breasted suit. Bow tie. His dark brown hair slicked straight back on his head, parted down the middle.

"Bryant, I'd like you to meet my campaign manager, Tiffany Meyer. I wanted to give her the opportunity to meet you before we left the studio."

Tiffany extended her hand to Bryant Grumble. "I want you to know I've admired your work for some time."

"Thanks, Tiffany. And I'm happy to say that I've also admired the way you're conducting Bill's campaign. And, I might add, it seems that it's beginning to pay off!"

Wilder broke in. "Tiffany, I'd also like you to meet my opponent tonight, Whyte Hunter."

She shook Hunter's hand. "I've heard a great deal about you, Dr. Hunter. It's good to finally meet you."

Hunter nodded.

Grumble finished the introductions: "Say, I'd like to introduce you two to my longtime friend here, Truman."

"Truman???"

"Yeah. Just "Truman." An unusual name for an unusual guy. Truman used to play middle linebacker for the Kansas City Chiefs. All pro for 7 straight years, weren't you, Truman?"

Truman nodded, but remained silent. He looked beyond Wilder directly into the eyes of Tiffany Meyer. Truman had already found and fixed on the person he perceived as his real opponent.

Grumble continued, "Truman's retired now. At least from football. Works as an external security executive for Badsworth and Hyde over in the Needle. So he's a colleague of Whyte's. Right, Truman?"

This time, Truman didn't even nod his head. His eyes remained locked with those of Tiffany Meyer.

Grumble noticed. "You two know each other or somethin?"

Tiffany responded. "No, Bryant. I've never had the pleasure of meeting Truman. Or shall I say Mr. Truman?"

She offered her hand. Truman took it and squeezed it, HARD. A squeeze that went unnoticed by the others, because it was nearly effortless on his part. He continued to look deeply into Tiffany's eyes. A chill went down her spine. She didn't like what she sensed in this man.

At all.

"Bill, we've got to be going. It's been a pleasure meeting you, Bryant. I hope Bill will have the opportunity to have both of us over for dinner at the White House some day."

"That's something I'll look forward to, Tiffany. It was nice meeting you both. Good luck with your campaign."

As they were preparing to leave the studio, Tiffany stopped Wilder. "What did you think of that guy Truman?"

"What do you mean? Seemed okay to me. You sense something?"

"I sure did. I've never met anyone who gave me such an instant case of the creeps. When I looked him in the eyes, I got the distinct feeling he knew everything there was to know about me, even though I don't know him from Adam."

"I'm sure you're just imagining things, Tiff."

"Well, I'm just as sure I'm not. And there's something else I'd like to know!"

"What?"

"What in blazes is an *external security executive?*"

PREMONITION OF DOOM

"Brighton Bellow? . . . The chairman of the board of Badsworth and Hyde wants to see me? . . . When? . . . He'll send a car? . . . Okay. I'll be here."

Tiffany Meyer hung up the phone and walked over to the desk in her hotel room at the New York Marriott. So Brighton Bellow wanted to talk to her. Chairman of the biggest investment banking firm in the world.

Brighton Bellow. . . . This guy took the title CEO seriously. He liked to be called "Chief," and was so addressed by most of his staff.

She knew why he wanted to talk. They didn't like what was going on in her campaign one bit. The investment banking interests had made no secret of their distaste for the proposed financial reforms of candidate Bill Wilder.

It was October 21, and Bill's plan had become a key item in the public's mind. Armed with Professor Mayer's intriguing ideas and specific proposals for limiting trading on SCARE, Bill's campaign had taken on a life of its own.

Badsworth and Hyde had even sponsored a series of antireform ads in local newspapers throughout the country. Recently they had even extended their campaign to television. But it wasn't working. It seemed that the public held investment bankers in lower esteem than they held politicians. The more they claimed that THE PLAN spelled disaster for the financial system and the economy, the more the public came to believe that there must be something right about his proposed reforms, given that B&H found it so distasteful. A case of the lady protesting too much.

And now the "Chief" wanted to see her. Did he really think that he could convince her of their position at this point in time? Surely that wasn't possible.

She had 45 minutes before Bellow's car would come for her. Time enough to catch a cup of coffee.

She put on her jacket, picked up her purse, and made her way out the door and onto the 51st floor balcony overlooking the expanse of the atrium, which ran all the way up from the lobby to the 60th floor.

At one end of the atrium were two twin towers, each supporting eight elevators. These elevators, however, were mounted on the outside of the towers. They were glass capsules, trimmed with lighted struts running from top to bottom. This old hotel had been erected years ago in the heart of the theater district. The struts reflected the lights trimming the many marquees that ran the length of Broadway.

The doors to the elevators were at the inside of the two towers. Tiffany walked along the balcony from her room to the entrance to one of the towers.

She hit the down button and waited for one of the eight doors surrounding her to respond.

"Ding."

The green light over one of the doors went on, indicating that the car was going down. She approached the door and entered the empty car as it opened. The door closed.

She hated elevators. When those doors closed, you were at their mercy. You could tell them where to go, but they were actually in control.

Tiffany hit "Lobby," and turned to face the atrium. She could see the elevators of the neighboring tower on the other side moving rapidly from floor to floor.

Hers had yet to move.

Tiffany hit "Lobby" a second time. She felt a nearly imperceptible move downward. Then a stop.

Now it *slipped!* It slipped about six inches, and then caught!

"God! ! !"

Sweat began to form on Tiffany's brow. The elevator was stopped still.

Tiffany reached again for "Lobby," but she stopped herself—should she?

What else could she do?

She hit the button a third time. This time she got a smooth response. The elevator was making its way to the bottom of the atrium.

"No wonder I hate these damn things!"

When she got out at the bottom, she made a mental note of the position of this particular elevator. "That's the last time I take a ride on you, Babe!"

Exiting the tower, she walked across the lobby bar to the gift shop, bought the *New York Times,* and walked next door to the coffee shop.

"One, please."

She followed the hostess to a table at the corner of the restaurant. Brightly lit—a good place to read her newspaper and have a cup of coffee.

"Would you like a menu?"

"No. Just coffee, please. Black."

Tiffany sipped her coffee and unfolded the paper, revealing the front page. She smiled.

The headline read, "Wilder Pulls into Second Place." The latest poll was out, and the news was good. Bill's support had risen to 30%, giving him a 2 percentage-point lead over the Republican candidate. He was only 3 points behind the Democrat. Within striking distance, with three weeks to go.

The headline story said this was the first time in modern history an independent had pulled ahead of a major party candidate. Wilder had momentum. He was committing few errors. With a little luck, his momentum could carry him into the White House.

Tiffany was so excited her cup rattled when she returned it to its saucer. Just a few more of the right cards to play, and her man would be president of the United States.

President.

After reading through the story two more times, she flipped through the rest of the paper for stories about the campaign.

There was no story on the final page of the first section, but there was an ad.

A full-page ad. Another message condemning financial reform from your friendly investment bankers at B&H.

The ad stated that Wilder's proposed reforms were tantamount to tinkering with the one segment of the economy that was arguably close to perfect in its operation. The contemplated reforms would most certainly reduce the level of liquidity in the stock market, resulting in an increase in the cost of capital and a lower level of capital spending, which would have a depressing effect on an economy that was sinking fast.

She was barely audible as she muttered, "What a bunch of garbage. Who do they think will believe this crap? This is the very *opposite* of the truth."

Actually, the ads were probably good for their campaign. If anything, these ads were probably increasing their support. "The stupid bankers at B&H are spending their money and actually contributing to our campaign."

Tiffany looked at her watch. Time for her rendezvous with Brighton Bellow. He, no doubt, was responsible for this ad.

She discarded the paper and made her way down to street level.

Parked in front of the hotel was the longest black limousine Tiffany had ever seen. Next to the back door stood a chauffeur dressed in a black uniform. Knowing who she was, he opened the door, and she climbed in.

The limo made its way down Broadway. In the distance she could see the approaching needle, reaching high into the sky.

Traffic was slow, but this gave Tiffany some time to examine the vehicle sent to deliver her to Brighton Bellow. The carpeting and leather were a matching steel blue. In front of her was a wet bar with a well-stocked refrigerator.

To the right was a set of six three-dimensional holographic monitors. She hit the power button, and all six turned on simultaneously. All were in living color, displaying images and security quotations in three-dimensional space. Each had a mouse capable of rotating the images to gain any perspective desired. If you didn't mind talking, the images also responded to vocal commands. The top three apparently displayed market statistics. Top left—statistics relating to the national economy on channels 1 through 5; relating to international markets on channels 6 to 10; relating to domestic, regional economies on channels 11 to 63. Top center—statistics relating to the income statements and balance sheets of domestic corporations. Top right—quotations from the major domestic and international markets. Bottom left—weather conditions throughout the world. The bottom center was apparently a closed-circuit network emanating from the bank or the banking system. Finally, on the bottom right, was plain old holographic TV (all channels, of course). Probably there to keep in tune with the pulse of the common man.

To the left of the bar, she found a communications system including three telephones, complete with telecommunication equipment.

Examining the rest of the interior, Tiffany found a small silver "button" mounted just behind the top of the rear seat. She was sure it was a microphone. The car was bugged. Its signal undoubtedly went straight to the bank.

The president of the United States didn't have a car this well equipped.

As they pulled up to the First America Tower, Tiffany noted the familiar figure of Truman waiting to greet her. He opened her door, she stepped out, and the limousine pulled away. Truman extended his hand toward the building, indicating that she should proceed through the doors of the main entrance, and Tiffany complied.

TOWER OF POWER

Truman followed her in. They rode the escalator to the second level, where they found the main entrance to the building's network of elevators. Truman led her to the right, away from the public elevators. Away from the lines of traffic formed by B&H's thousands of middle managers and staff. They approached a security center.

What the public could see of B&H's Security System was the familiar airport arrangement, only somewhat more elaborate. Truman approached the individual in charge, a very large man with a pockmarked face. Sitting behind the counter, the man nodded and picked up his telephone.

"Tiffany Meyer is here to see Mr. Bellow."

After receiving instructions he motioned Truman to proceed to the security check on the right. Her purse was x-rayed, and she was asked to pass through a metal detector. Good thing she had forgotten to wear the 30-caliber submachine gun, which she usually kept strapped to her right leg!!! Tiffany mumbled, "What are they afraid of up there, anyway?"

One of the female security officers heard her and responded. "I'm told that we had some trouble with demonstrators back in the ought-years."

"I don't see any demonstrators around here today!"

"It's B&H policy, Ma'am."

Having passed her security check, Tiffany was escorted by Truman to the set of four elevators reaching the highest floors of the bank. One was open. They entered.

Truman hit "95." The door closed, and they began a smooth ascent to their destination. In less than a minute, the doors opened to reveal the hall extending to the office of Brighton Bellow. The first thing Tiffany noticed was that "95" was actually two floors in one. The ceiling was more than 30 feet above the floor.

At the end of the hall, Truman opened one of the two 20-foot doors leading to Bellow's office. A receptionist waited. She rose to greet the person summoned by Brighton Bellow. Her voice was cold. "Mr. Bellow is expecting you. Please come this way."

Two more 20-foot doors. The receptionist opened one, and Tiffany walked in. This was unbelievable. Across 100 feet of room, Bellow sat behind his desk. And behind him was the most incredible span of window she had ever seen.

Bellow rose and walked over to greet her.

"Typical Wall Street type," she thought. Dark gray pinstriped suit, paisley tie, black wing-tip shoes, hair perfectly in place, at midpoint on its journey from dark brown to white.

Tiffany's 5'9" seemed to tower over Bellow's 5'5".

This man seemed to be dominated by his ROOM.

Tiffany received Bellow's extended hand. "I'm happy you accepted my invitation to chat. I've been wanting to meet you for some time."

Me? Tell me. Why would you want to meet me and not my *candidate?*"

"We have been watching you and your candidate for some time. You have conducted an excellent campaign. *You* are to be congratulated. *You* should be proud of yourself. You seem to have made all the right moves."

"We have come a long way. And it does seem like we may come away with the grand prize after all, doesn't it?"

"*Indeed!* In fact, that is why you are here today."

"Not surprising. If we were running a distant third, I doubt we'd capture your interest at all, would we?"

"Let me assure you, Ms. Meyer, there is very *little* that escapes my interest. Your campaign has disturbed me from the very beginning, even when you *were* running a distant third."

Tiffany smiled and walked over to the biggest window in the world.

"Nice view."

With her back to Bellow, "Been watching us from up here, have you? And I take it you don't like our platform."

"We don't like your platform, Ms. Meyer. We don't like the prospect of an unprecedented change in the structure of the American financial system—a change that will ultimately cause serious harm to the country."

Tiffany knew the dramatic impact Wilder's proposed reforms would have on Bellow's operations. But she decided to bait him, nevertheless.

"Exaggerating a bit, aren't you, Mr. Bellow? After all, insofar as they affect your firm, our plans only call for limitations on trading activity in the stock market."

"The stock market is the one institution in this country that runs as smoothly as a clock. It's the most perfectly competitive market in the capitalistic system. It doesn't need to be fixed by your plans. It's perfectly fine running the way it is."

"If you call the history of the last 8 months smooth, I'd hate to ride on your roller coaster."

Bellow felt the need to turn the dial down. He walked over to his desk and buzzed his secretary.

"Ellen. Ask Dr. Hunter to come in, please."

"What's been going on in the stock market merely reflects what's been going on in the economy. We at B&H are as concerned about that as anyone. In fact, I'm sure you know that we have much more to lose than most. With capital spending dropping as fast as it has, our investment banking division has been doing poorly indeed. Revenues are down nearly 30%."

"What about your revenues from SCARE? I've read that's been up by more than 50%."

"Can't deny that. But that's the reason I've asked you to join us here today. I'd like you to come to a better understanding of what you're dealing. . . . Whyte! Whyte. Thanks for joining us. I'd like you to meet Tiffany Meyer, Bill Wilder's campaign manager."

Whyte Hunter approached the window and extended his hand to Tiffany.

"We've already met, Brighton. Nice to see you again, Tiffany."

Recalling her last handshake in his presence, Tiffany reluctantly accepted his greeting.

"Whyte, I'd like you to introduce Tiffany to some of the features of SCARE. It's my feeling that if she comes to understand the network better, she'll come to appreciate it, much as we do."

Releasing Tiffany's hand, Hunter swept his in an arc toward the south end of the room. "Come with us, and I'll show you some of the more interesting features of SCARE."

Tiffany walked south. That end of the room had a distinctly different feel to it. As if walking from the 19th to the 21st century. The entire south wall was a checkerboard of monitors surrounding an 80-inch center screen. The monitors were filled with graphs and tables. Many of the graphs were moving in real time.

Hunter approached the displays and spoke to the computer. "Trading System please." Instantly, the center monitor displayed an array of options.

Hunter turned to Tiffany. "This system links our investors directly to SCARE. Portfolio managers can analyze their positions and make appropriate modifications with unprecedented economy and efficiency. Let me show you. I'll bring up the current holding of one of our clients." Turning back to the display, "The current holdings of Tynex, please."

Tiffany considered the irony of being polite to a computer. It was almost as if the machines were becoming human.

The center monitor displayed an array of holdings by asset class and dollar amount—domestic stocks, international stocks, bonds, real estate, etc.

Hunter made his selection. "Domestic stocks."

The monitor now displayed a complete listing of the 86 domestic stock holdings of Tynex. The amount held. The price. And the rate of return for each over the previous day, month, quarter, and year.

"Characteristics."

The numbers to the right of each stock changed. Hunter explained that the numbers showed the sensitivities of each stock to different aspects of economic activity.

"Ford Motor Company."

Ford now filled the screen. "For example, Ford has a Long Bond beta of 0.70. This means that if the rate of return to the standard long-term Treasury bond goes up by 1%, you can expect Ford's stock to rise in price by 0.7%."

Tiffany surveyed the list of other "betas," each showing how Ford could be expected to respond to particular aspects of the economy and the financial markets.

"Now watch this. Suppose you have a concern about higher inflation, and you want to see how your current stockholdings might respond to an inflating economy. . . ."

"Consumer Price Index."

The center monitor now displayed a graph showing, on the left-hand side, a history of the rate of inflation for the previous year. On the right-hand side was a computer projection of inflation in the future. Hunter walked up to the terminal and superimposed, with a mouse, a projection of more rapid future inflation.

"Monte Carlo Simulation of Future Portfolio Value."

The center monitor began to dance. One after another, time-series of possible future paths that Tynex's equity portfolio might take, in the hypothesized inflating environment, were momentarily displayed on the screen. Each left a trace shadow, showing its path, as it was replaced by the next. After showing several hundred simulated possibilities, the monitor displayed the most likely outcome surrounded by confidence bands.

Hunter turned to Tiffany. "That's what's likely to happen to Tynex if inflation takes hold. Now for what Tynex should do about it."

"Scenario-consistent trades, please."

The monitor now displayed a list of trade recommendations. Stocks that should be pared from Tynex's list and stocks that should be bought to put Tynex's pension fund in the best possible position for dealing with an inflating environment.

"All I would have to do now is give the computer the instructions to execute the trades. The trades would be instantly executed by SCARE at a penny per share. It's as simple as that."

"Active market please."

The graphic that Professor Mayer had called up in his office now appeared on the screen. The value for the S&P 500 in real time. The graph that was available 24 hours a day, on channel 200, on every television set in the civilized world. The S&P 500 was moving with alarming volatility.

Hunter frowned. "Hmm. . . . Looks like the volatility's up again, Brighton. Let's check on it.

"Term-structure of volatility please." A bar graph now appeared on the screen. The 20 bars showed the projected level of stock market volatility for the next 20 quarters. The current level of volatility was at 80%. The graphic indicated that volatility was projected to fall at a decreasing rate to 40% by the final quarter. Over the next 2 years, it was projected to average 70%.

Tiffany's interest level had risen dramatically. "Tell me, how do you project what the volatility will be in the quarter after this one?"

Hunter replied, "That's not our projection; it's the market's. Those are implied volatilities computed from the prices of call options on the S&P 500."

"I know about implied volatilities, but how do you compute the volatility for the second quarter from today's option prices?"

"Well, the options have different maturities. The price of a one-quarter option reflects the expected level of volatility over the next quarter. The price of a two-quarter option reflects the average level of volatility over the next two quarters. By looking at the difference between the two volatilities, we can compute what volatility is expected to be in the second quarter."

"Clever. But I see by your projections that the market is beginning to feel that high volatility is going to be sticking around for awhile."

"That's true. Things are beginning to look increasingly uncertain for the economy. The market's beginning to project that for the longer term."

"If you ask me, the market's more concerned about its own behavior than about what's going on in the economy. If you ask me, the market—and more specifically, your market—is the principal problem."

Hunter smiled. "I think you've been talking to too many of these behavioral finance types. There's nothing wrong with the stock market. If you realized that, you wouldn't be out there campaigning against us, trying to put constraints on the operations of SCARE."

"Your opinions wouldn't be influenced by the fact that our constraints would probably cut deeply into the $60 billion in annual revenue you guys take in from SCARE, would they?"

Brighton Bellow broke his silence. "Our profitability is not our main concern, Ms. Meyer. B&H has maintained its profitability throughout this century and through most of the last two. We will continue to be profitable in the future, with or without your reforms."

Tiffany was puzzled. She turned and walked over to confront Bellow. "If it's not profits that you're worried about, then what is it, Mr. Bellow?"

"The issue is *control,* Ms. Meyer. The issue is who is to hold the reins to the economy. We have always held those reins. We will continue to hold them in the future."

"*You* control the economy?"

"Ms. Meyer, there are two basic types of economies operating in the world today. Most are capitalistic. A very few remain socialistic. In a socialistic economy, the central government decides how resources are to be allocated between demands. How much is to be consumed. How much is to be invested for the future. What is to be produced now. What will be produced in the future.

"In a capitalistic economy, these decisions are made by markets. And there is one market that is central to these decisions. That is the market for capital. And the cornerstone of that market is the stock market. The goods and services that sustain us are the final products of investments financed through the stock market. Firms that believe they have the right answers to the future needs and desires of the American consumer go to the stock market to raise the capital they need to put their plans in motion. The companies with the best ideas get capital at the best prices. Bad ideas aren't financed; good ones are. No need for central planning here. The ideas that command the best prices in the capital market are the ones that ultimately get financed."

"By the best, of course, you mean the most profitable ideas."

"The most profitable ideas are usually the best ideas, Ms. Meyer."

"Love Canal was profitable, but as an idea, it wasn't exactly sterling, was it?"

"The capitalistic system isn't a perfect system, but it is the best system, nonetheless."

Bellow continued. "B&H has, in the past, concentrated on the supply side of the capital market. For centuries now, we have helped the stock and bond issues of firms seeking the fruition of their good ideas. With SCARE, and the systems Whyte has been showing you, we have now moved to the demand side of the capital market, where the investors are. By putting the proper technology into the hands of these investors, by increasing the ease and lowering the costs of trading, we are making capital cheaper for the firms with the good ideas.

"More than that. . . . By operating on both sides of the market we extend our span of control over the very center of the market economy. Control, Ms. Meyer. That is what this firm is, and has been, about.

"Whyte, if you will excuse us, I have something to show Ms. Meyer."

"But of course. It's been delightful, Tiffany."

"Thanks for the tour, Dr. Hunter."

Tiffany followed Bellow as he crossed the room to another pair of 20-foot doors. Bellow opened one of them. The light from the office penetrated the blackened room, revealing a long table. Based on the continuity of the grain, it was apparently made from a single gigantic ebony tree.

She preceded him into the room, as Bellow hit the lights that would help him to make his point—lights illuminating the portraits of him and those who had come before him.

Bellow walked past the table to the far end of the room.

He pointed above him to a picture of a man with one of the biggest pot-bellies Tiffany had ever seen. The man had red hair, long sideburns, and an orange mustache. He was standing beside a red leather chair.

"This is Christian Badsworth, the founder of this firm in 1836. At that time, B&H was a commercial bank. Christian started everything, not only for this firm but for this country as well. He helped finance much of the railroad track that pushed the frontier to the Pacific. This bank helped Jay Gould and Jim Fisk convert legitimate bonds into worthless Erie Railroad stock certificates so they could sell them to Cornelius Vanderbilt back in 1867."

Bellow waited for a reaction. None came. He walked around the table, past four more former directors. "These are the men who molded this country into a world power. They financed the stringing of line—electric lines, telegraph lines, and finally telephone lines, from city to city and from state to state. Gilton Morrison over here helped rebuild most of the city of Chicago after the fire."

Tiffany Meyer nodded and responded with an obligatory "Very interesting."

Bellow moved to the next picture. "Jonathan Goldfellow. He assumed power in 1910. With his help and guidance, Henry Ford began producing automobiles on the first assembly line, and Thomas Benoist started the first commercial airline between St. Petersburg and Tampa."

Five more steps down the line. "In 1925, Goldfellow handed the flag to Martin Billingsly. Under Billingsly, the bank helped fuel the great bull market of '27, '28 and '29. And, in addition, to this very day, this man holds the industry record for taking firms through the most major bankruptcies in a single fiscal year—87 in 1931."

"An impressive accomplishment indeed."

"I sense that you're really not very impressed, Ms. Meyer, but let me tell you something. In a bankruptcy, we have a transfer of ownership, a transfer of control. This firm ultimately determines the identity of both parties in such a transfer. And, of course, we're not talking about small amounts of money. We're talking about major industrial firms and who owns and controls them. We deal in control. We determine who holds the reins."

Tiffany remained unresponsive.

Bellow seemed to become discouraged. "In any case, let's move on." His next stop was Scheffield Tempermann, who took over in 1939.

"You may have thought that the United States government financed World War II, but it was actually Scheffield who had the biggest influence in determining exactly which manufacturers would bid successfully for the contracts to build all the battleships, bombers, and guns the federal government needed to fight the war."

They had now nearly come full circle around the table, face to face with Bellow's immediate predecessor, Schenley Harrington, who it seems was single-handedly responsible for laying the interstate highway system. And now for Brighton Bellow himself.

"And what about you, Mr. Bellow? How have you extended your influence over American industry?"

"Under my tenure, the firm has financed much of the search for new sources of energy, including more efficient techniques for extracting the old sources, coal and oil. We also were a major player in the explosion in ultra micro processing. But, in my opinion, when all the dust settles, I will be known for the major restructuring that's continuing in corporate Asia. This bank has helped finance and execute 93 takeovers in the last 3 years alone. And we helped finance 27 successful attempts to fend off raiders as well."

"You determine who is in *control*."

"That's precisely correct, Ms. Meyer. We determine who holds the power —who holds the reins."

"Through your activity on both sides of the financial market."

"To accomplish anything in a capitalistic society, you've got to have money. We control the capital. We have the financing. We help establish the prices. And, as a result, we determine who gets to produce and who does not."

Tiffany took a step closer to Bellow. "So the issue is control and power. You don't want us messing around with your control of the financial markets."

The light illuminating his portrait cast Brighton Bellow in dark silhouette. "Of course the issue is control. We control the amount and nature of corporate investment. We decide whether to invest or not to invest. We decide how much to invest and, ultimately, how to invest."

"We determine which new products are introduced and which never see the light of day. In the final analysis, our firm determines the quality of the environment and the quality of health care in this country. Through our control of the economy, we direct the movement of populations from area to area. We determine which firms are taken over and which management teams are displaced. We determine the fate of ethnic groups fighting for power in Europe and the ultimate fate of the governments that try to resist them."

Bellow stopped for a pregnant pause. "And, we also determine the outcome of *political campaigns* here in the United States."

"Well, Mr. Bellow, you don't seem to be successfully determining the outcome of *this* one, do you? Although I surely can't fault you for not trying your *best*. But you see our organization isn't short of funds. We have *plenty* of money to get us through the last week of the campaign. We don't need financing. And we don't have to take *your* advice on how to run *our* campaign."

A strange expression came over Bellow's face. It reminded her of the expression on Truman's face nearly 2 months before; she felt a distinct chill.

"This campaign is not over, Ms. Meyer, and we have not *yet* tried our *best*."

Tiffany deliberately stepped directly into Brighton Bellow's *personal space.* He stepped back. She moved in again. He stepped back again, this time behind one of the blood-red leather chairs lining the conference table.

From the other side of the chair, she held him with her eyes. She penetrated *deep* into his brain, grabbed it from inside, and squeezed hard.

Then slowly and precisely, she gave him his answer. "Why? Why should I be intimidated by you or your firm? As far as I'm concerned, your comments have been outrageous and ridiculous. You are ridiculous!!! I've given you all the consideration I'm going to, thank you."

Tiffany had one weakness. Her temper. And it was about to get the best of her once again.

"And you, Mr. Bellow. I'm looking at you right now. I'm looking into you right now. And do you know what I see? I see a little man. A man I don't respect. A man I'm not the *least* bit afraid of. Because I'm smarter than you. Do you know that? And what's more, I'm better than you. I may not have your power, but I can live with myself when I go to sleep at night. I sleep like a baby. Do you???"

Bellow was taken back by the *fire* in her eyes, the *conviction* in her voice and the *force* of her comments. He hadn't overestimated this one.

"Ms. Meyer, I seem to have offended you somehow. I think you must have misunderstood something. I didn't mean to imply that I, or the rest of my colleagues pictured in this room, are unusually distinguished individuals. The power here does not reside in us. It resides in the organization that, itself, resides in this *building*. To a great extent, the 10 of us rose to the top on the basis of political accident and chance happening. There are many people in this organization who would fit nicely into this position. Who, in fact, may be more suitable than I."

Tiffany loosened her grip on his brain—slightly.

"But Ms. Meyer, please don't *underestimate* the scope of the *power* that resides here. You, or at least your candidate, are on the verge of ascending to a position of great power. Some say the president of the United States is the most powerful individual in the world. But listen carefully when I tell you that they are *wrong*. They do not know what power *really is.*"

"Are you trying to tell me that *your* power transcends that of the *presidency?*"

"Again, Ms. Meyer, we're not talking about *my* power. We're talking about the power of this firm. And, yes, do not underestimate this power even relative to that of the presidency. If you find this hard to believe, consider the *enormous* influence this firm has had on the growth and development of this *country.*"

Tiffany was becoming angry again.

"Well, Mr. Bellow, go ahead and exercise that power. Run your advertisements. Lobby your congressmen. Do what you wish. You will affect neither the course of our campaign or our platform. Is that clear?"

"You're making yourself quite clear, Ms. Meyer. Quite clear indeed. You must do what you must do, and we must respond accordingly." Bellow walked back into his office. "In any case, it's been an enlightening discussion. I'll have Truman show you the way back to your hotel."

OPERATION POISON PILL

Friday, November 4, and the election was only 4 days away. The breeze blew gently through Tiffany's long, honey-blond hair. The sun was ablaze, and it was unusually warm for November. Great day for a political rally, and they had a terrific turnout to match.

Tiffany surveyed the crowd. There had to be at least 40,000 people out there. There hadn't been a crowd this size in Central Park since the Brook Parker concert back in the 2010s.

They had the lead. The latest poll said they were up by 3 percentage points over the Democrat. Their lead over the Republican had increased to 10 points. Apparently, Bill was pulling most of his votes from him.

Tiffany was sitting toward the back of the speaker's platform to the left of Bill Wilder, who was having little trouble drumming up enthusiasm in the crowd.

"My fellow Americans, today we face the specter of chaos in the world's stock markets—chaos that is leading our economy ever closer to a state of collapse. Ever closer to a second Great Depression. My opponent has a solution. He says that you, *the American taxpayer,* are the real problem. It's you. You see, *you're* not paying enough taxes. He thinks you have *too much money.* He wants you to pay *more.* Well, I ask you. Do you think you have *too much money? Do* you?"

A roar from the crowd. "NO!!!"

"Of course you don't. He must have his head in the sand. Anyone who's been half-awake would know that our paychecks have fallen off a cliff. And he wants to clip some more off your check.

"But *I* say that *you're* not the problem. I say we've got to look to where this chaos began—in the stock market. We can't tame the *economy* until we tame the *stock market.*"

Wilder's comments continued to draw momentous cheers from the crowd. For them, the choice was easy. More regulation over more taxes!

Nothing could stop them now. Bill Wilder was on his way to the White House.

The White House!

Tiffany wondered what Brighton Bellow was thinking at this very moment. He undoubtedly was wringing his hands in frustration and fear. She knew where he was. Looking out his window at the top of the Needle. She turned to the west, and there it was. Looming over them, forever watching.

The west was to Bill's left on the other side of the stand. Standing right next to the platform was the large man with the pockmarked face she had seen at the security desk at the First America Tower. He was talking into what appeared to be a very small two-way radio. Judging from the look on his face, and the animated way he was speaking into the instrument, the man was clearly excited about something. He was looking to his left.

Tiffany looked in that direction, and after some searching made out another man equipped with the same type of radio. Then, off to her far right, away from the crowd, still another man with still another radio. Off in the distance, she thought she could spot two other men with radios as well.

By this point, she had become accustomed to seeing a member of the First America Security Force in the crowds addressed by Wilder. Usually Truman. But in the past, she'd never seen more than one at a time. Now, suddenly, here were *five*. At least. If she could spot five from up here, there were probably many more.

Why???

"My fellow Americans, you have a clear choice in this election. You say you want to rid your children of the burden of the deficit? Well, you can vote for my Democratic opponent who wants to raise your taxes. Or you can vote for me. I want to eliminate the deficit by sending this economy in the right direction. And I will do this, not by raising your taxes, but rather by changing the structure of the financial system. This change will leave that system more financially sound. This change will stabilize the American economy. This is your choice. I ask you now, what is your response?"

This was Bill's key line. And now came the familiar chant from the crowd.

"WILDER . . . WILDER . . . WILDER . . ."

Bill was really working this crowd into a frenzy, but Tiffany was more concerned with radio-equipped external security executives.

She was sure that something important was going to happen soon. And there was only one way to find out what.

She must return to the Needle.

Tiffany walked behind the backdrop of the platform, where her assistant Jed Hirsch was talking to a pair of reporters.

She interrupted him. "Jed, I want you to come with me. We've got to go over to the B&H Tower."

"I'll be done here in a minute, Tiff."

"I'm sorry, Jed; we've got to go right now. I'm afraid there's no time to waste."

"You've got it, Tiff. But what's the big rush?"

En route to the Needle, Tiffany explained her concern over the large number of external security executives in the crowd.

"But what could they be up to? They've been watching us from the beginning, but I'd figured it was harmless enough."

"You may be right. But I've got a real bad feeling about all this, and I'm going to get to the bottom of it right now."

They jumped into a cab, and rode to the other side of the park.

Upon entering the Needle, the pair approached the security desk. Tiffany spotted Truman next to the X-ray machine. He noticed her as well, and walked over in time to hear Tiffany say to the woman behind the desk, "My name is Tiffany Meyer, and this is my assistant, Jed Hirsch. We must see Brighton Bellow immediately."

Peering over rimless glasses, "You must be mistaken, Miss. Mr. Bellow is usually booked solid for requested appointments at least 2 weeks in advance."

Truman touched the woman's shoulder and nodded his approval for the meeting. The woman picked up the telephone, "Tiffany Meyer to see Mr. Bellow." After a moment's pause and through tight lips, "I guess I was wrong. You've been cleared to go up."

The fact that she had such immediate access to Bellow only served to increase Tiffany's concerns.

After passing through the security screens, Tiffany and her assistant followed Truman to the elevators.

Tiffany turned her back to Truman, and whispered to her assistant, "Jed, you wait down here for me. If I'm not back within 20 minutes, I want you to call the police. Understand?"

Jed rubbed his brow, and responded in a low voice. "Tiff, are you sure you really want me to call the police?"

"Yes, Jed, call the police!"

"Okay, the police—20 minutes."

Tiffany boarded the elevator with Truman. He hit "95," and they were on their way.

BAD FELLOW BELLOW

"Good afternoon, Ms. Meyer. I'm surprised to see you. What brings you here today? I thought we'd finished our conversation last week."

"I thought so too Mr. Bell. . . . Do you mind if I call you Brighton?"

"Why not. Come over here. I'll pour you some of the best French cognac you've ever tasted."

Bellow seemed to be celebrating something.

He walked over to his bar, built into the wall to the left of the biggest window in the world. Tiffany followed him. As they approached the bar, Tiffany noticed a memorandum Bellow had apparently been reading and had temporarily left next to the sink. Across its top, it read in large letters:

STRICTLY CONFIDENTIAL

She couldn't quite make out the contents of the memo, even with her 20/10 vision. She needed to get closer, so she stepped into Bellow's personal space once again.

Again, he moved back, blocking her view of the memorandum.

She *had* to get him to shift position.

Tiffany walked over to the south end of the office. Displayed on the center monitor was the bar graph of implied volatilities for the next 20 quarters. Tiffany noted with alarm that the market was now projecting volatility to settle at a level of *50%* over the long-term. That was an increase of 10% from the last time she had looked at the graph. This was *not* good news. As it had in the 1930s, the long-term cost of equity capital—the hurdle rate for capital investment—was rising, and the whole country was becoming preoccupied with the stock market.

Even as Bellow followed her to the south end of his office, Tiffany retraced her steps and walked back to the bar.

Tiffany now had a clear view of the memorandum. It read:

"OPERATION POISON PILL is scheduled for completion on 4 November, immediately following the political rally in Central Park."

POISON PILL? What was *that*? The rally was obviously Bill's. POISON PILL was connected to Bill. Those men in the park are connected to OPERATION POISON PILL. But what is the meaning of POISON PILL?

Bellow moved back, and the memorandum disappeared from view. He poured two generous brandies, and gave one to Tiffany. They walked back to his desk. Bellow sat behind it, sipping his brandy. Tiffany took note of the engraved nameplate sitting atop Bellow's desk. It read:

THE CHIEF

"So Tiffany, tell me. What is it that I can do for you?"

"I'd like to talk some more about the impact of our proposals on SCARE. I'd like to talk about a possible *reconciliation* of our interests."

"Tiffany, as far as I'm concerned, we are already reconciled. We know your man is the likely winner of this election. That's obvious by now. Now it's up to the firm to learn how to live under his new system."

This, again, made Tiffany uneasy. An abrupt turnabout just wasn't in the cards.

"Then you've accepted all aspects of our proposals?"

"In business, any business, you've got to be flexible. You've got to be able to adapt to changing situations. Animal life, for example, that fails to adapt to changes in its environment, inevitably becomes extinct. As times change, situations change. If our firm is to survive, it must change with the times."

Tiffany didn't believe any of this for a minute. "Brighton, *such* a change of attitude in only a *few* short days! Tell me, how is B&H going to adapt?"

"We're going to raise our prices. In the future, it will cost 3 cents a share to trade."

Tiffany's eyes were again inside Bellow's brain. What a bunch of *crap!* Did he really expect her to believe this line? B&H simply wouldn't be able to meet the competition at 3 cents a share!

"We're also going to be emphasizing activities in our merger and acquisition division. You know. Designing takeover and defense strategies—golden parachutes, green mail, poison pills. . . . All those sorts of things."

Bingo!!!

"Poison pills? What is a poison pill anyway?"

"A poison pill is just a term used in the investment banking industry. It's a strategy used to ward off or *terminate* a raider."

Tiffany's eyes widened. Hold it now . . . relax . . . don't signal alarm.

As unbelievable as it seemed, they were going to assassinate Bill. . . . Probably at the end of the rally.

There was barely enough time to warn him. She had to get out of the building without alarming Bellow. *Get your eyes out of Bellow's brain.* Visual communication goes two ways. Look anywhere. Look at his *big nose,* for God's sake.

But Tiffany's reaction hadn't gone unnoticed. Bellow turned from her toward the direction of the bar where he saw the memorandum he had mistakenly left for *anyone* to see. What a *shameful* mistake he had made! He was *completely* unnerved. His face reddened two shades.

Tiffany noticed his reaction. She *had* to get out of there.

Now.

"I'm relieved that you have accepted our proposals. Bill will be happy to hear that. I'm anxious to get back to him to tell him."

Bellow composed himself. "Very well. I'll have Truman show you out."

"That's quite all right. This is my second visit. I can find my way out by *myself,* thank you."

"*Nonsense,* Tiffany. Truman will be *more* than happy to escort such a beautiful woman to the door."

Tiffany followed Bellow out the doors of his office to his receptionist's chamber, where Truman was waiting for her.

Bellow walked to the door leading to the hall and opened it.

He looked slyly at Truman. "Truman, would you please be so kind as to escort Ms. Meyer to her *final* destination?"

At the door, Truman stood to the right, Bellow to the left. Tiffany had 8 feet between her and the open door.

And she had a plan.

She first removed one pump and then the other.

Barefoot, she spoke as seductively as possible.

"Brighty, you can't let me go without showing you why I really came up here. Can you, Brighty?"

She began sliding the tight skirt of her suit up her long, shapely legs. Brighton Bellow was absolutely astonished! Both men stood there completely transfixed. From behind her, Tiffany heard Bellow's receptionist exclaim, "*Oh, my God!*"

Tiffany got the skirt up to her hips. *Now!!!* In a split second, she bolted past both men and out the door.

"For God's sake, *catch her,* Truman. She knows about POISON PILL!!!"

Showing his prowess as a former middle linebacker, Truman bolted after her, as though she were Walter Payton heading for his end zone. Now running in the "open field," she had no more than 4 steps on her pursuer. Her zeal for physical fitness was about to pay off!

Four steps and 100 feet between her and the elevator at the end of the hall.

There, a small investment banker stood midway between the four elevator doors waiting for one to open. The call button was on.

Seventy-five feet to go. The gap was now only *3* steps.

Tiffany could see one of the center doors open. The small man stepped in, turned around, and punched his floor. Now, for the first time, he became aware of the spectacle coming in his direction. A beautiful woman bearing down on him, skirt hiked up around her waist, running surely as fast as he'd ever seen a woman run. A hulk of a man in pursuit. Amazingly, he seemed to be gaining on her, even though he was more than twice her size. And all this was bearing down directly on *him.* Should he hold the elevator? *Or get the hell out of there as fast as possible?*

Twenty feet to go, a 2-step lead, *and the damn elevator door was starting to close.*

One chance. If she touched either of those closing doors, she knew they would re-open, giving Truman all the time he needed. She had to get through without touching them.

Only 4 steps to the door, but no more breathing room. Just as Truman reached for the back of her collar, she started her dive, turning her body in flight as she approached the closing doors. The little man stepped aside as she sailed through, left side down. The doors barely touched the tips of her toes as they sealed.

Outside, Truman's hulk *smashed* against the seal just as her head hit the red leather padding at the rear of the elevator. Happily, she could feel her body hit the floor. She was conscious. And going up.

She smiled at the little man who had obviously never been through an experience like this before. "You don't mind if I hitch a ride with you, do you?"

"Well, I'm only going up two floors, but, ya know, that's as far as this one goes anyway."

"Good enough for me, Mister."

Tiffany picked herself off the floor and looked at the scrape on her left forearm. Red as a beet, but no pain yet. She left her skirt hiked up. Truman wouldn't give up that easily.

As they rose toward the 97th floor, the little man gave her the once over. He wanted to ask . . . , but held his silence until the door re-opened at 97.

"If I might ask . . ."

"Mister, I'm afraid I *really* don't have the time."

She hit the button for 95. That would send this car back down to Truman, who had undoubtedly hit the up button on that floor. Then she jumped out almost as fast as she had leaped in.

As soon as the doors closed, she hit the down button and waited for the next elevator to come up. The little banker was fascinated. He just stood there watching her.

To her right was the stairwell. She approached it, opened the door, and listened. Voices. Steps. Men running up to 97. They hadn't waited for the elevator. She quickly closed the door and ran back to the elevators.

Open. *Please. . . .*

Now. . . .

Now. . . .

"Ding."

The down light on the extreme left elevator turned on, and Tiffany ran to its door. She looked to the stairwell. She could hear sound through the door.

The doorknob turned.

The stairwell and elevator doors opened in concert. Truman ran out as Tiffany stepped in. She hit LOBBY, and *prayed* for a quick close.

She got it. Tiffany smiled broadly as Truman's body once again hit the sealed door.

From outside: "Blast it!"

What do you know about that? *Truman can talk!!! "Going down, Truman."*

"96, 95, please don't stop, 94, 93, . . . 87, 86" but now it was slowing down.

It stopped *dead,* lights out. It was pitch black and silent in the car.

Tiffany groped for the buttons. She found the one most likely to be LOBBY and pressed it. Nothing. She pressed the one next to it. Nothing. No power.

Trapped.

"I don't believe this." She had put herself precisely in the position they wanted her in. They had her on ice until they finished with Bill. Then they would bring her back up to the 95th floor for disposal. Bill was done for and, given that, so was she.

Black and silent.

Almost silent, anyway. She could hear sounds coming from elevators. It seems they had only cut the power to hers.

If she could only *change elevators. . . .*

Tiffany explored the walls of the car with her hands. Above the padding that had saved her head, if not her neck, was a metal railing. It extended the length of the back wall as well as the two sides. She knew that on the ceiling of nearly every elevator was an escape door.

She reached up, but couldn't touch the ceiling. Then she jumped and reached it easily. She kept jumping until her fingers felt a ridge. Inside the ridge was a recessed area that surely enclosed the escape door. With a series of jumps, she carefully determined the position of the escape door relative to the elevator walls.

Pressing her back to one of the rear corners of the elevator, she grabbed the rails with both hands. She pulled one foot up and propped it securely on the rail, inside her grip. Keeping her back and head pressed against the corner, she did the same thing with her other foot. In the same motion, she extended her squat and fell forward while reaching *desperately* for the recessed area.

She found it in time to break her fall.

With her feet on the rail and one hand braced against the recessed wall, she pushed up against the escape door. It didn't give. Push *harder.* It opened. She popped it and pushed it aside. Through the door, she could see light.

Gripping the ledge outside with both hands, Tiffany abandoned her foothold on the rails, pulling up enough to get an elbow out. It was her scraped forearm, and it burned. Now the other forearm.

Her head was fully out of the elevator. The acrid smell of metal and grease permeated the air. It was an easy matter to pull her body up to a sitting position, legs still inside the escape door. Time to take her bearings.

She was in the very bowels of the Needle.

This was an eerie scene. On the uppermost floors there were only 4 elevators. But at this level, there were at least 12 abreast. She could see 3 of the other cars. One was six shafts away and 3 floors above, on its way up. Another was in the seventh shaft, far below, and going down. The third was in the very next shaft over, stationary, 3 floors above her.

Each car had its own set of eight external lights at its corners. Lights also emerged from within the building itself through door after door stacked down each shaft as far as she could see. Her car was stuck between 84 and 85. The car was flush against the shaft on the door side; 2 feet separated the rear of the car from the rear of the shaft. The two sides of the car, however, faced wide-open space.

A better view would help. Tiffany pulled her legs from the escape door and tried to get on her feet to look down. She was up for less than a second before retreating to her knees. Her heart pounded fiercely as the shaft spun round and round.

Sitting securely on the top of the car, she gradually inched her way toward its edge, her legs dangling in open space.

Normally, heights didn't bother her, but something about this was different. The hollowed shaft *seemed to have no bottom.* At least, none that she could see. As she looked down, the 10 feet separating the front and back walls faded to a point and then completely disappeared. It was nearly a thousand feet to the floor, and the 10 feet of bottom was invisible from way up here.

It seemed like you could fall *forever.* . . .

Tiffany Meyer felt her fear turn to paralysis. Her skin turned cold and clammy. She was incapable of movement. A move, any move, would surely send her over the side. She just couldn't move. She couldn't even think. But she wanted *out* of this shaft. *Real bad.*

SNAP . . . WHIRRRRRRR. . . . She snapped her head up in the direction of the sound. The elevator in the next shaft was on its way down—*fast.* She'd had no idea they moved that fast.

Paralysis gave way to panic as she realized the three inches that would soon separate the cars *left no room for her legs.* She swung them up and around just in time to allow the car free passage on its way down.

It came to a stop a floor and a half below.

And as soon as it stopped, she realized the terrifying solution to her problem.

She could *jump* to that car, enter its escape door, and ride it down to the lobby.

She could *jump* to that car. . . .

She could *jump.* . . .

Come on! If she couldn't even stand on this one, *how in blazes could she jump to that one?*

What else? Crawl back in the hole and wait to be transported to her fate on "95"? She *must* jump. . . .

Tiffany swung her legs back over the edge and inched forward. Now another inch, and another, until she could feel her body approach that precise point where it would stop gripping and begin slipping. *The point of no return.* She wasn't there yet, but she was damn close. Just a matter of will.

She should jump. . . .

Let's go the final inch. Let's get this over with.

And now the Needle was going to kill her.

SNAP . . . WHIRRRRRRRR. . . .

Oh my God, no!!!!

The elevator below was on its way down again!!! Receding from her.

Hold it! ! !

But Tiffany had already passed her point of no return. She was over the edge. No longer sitting on the nice, solid elevator. *She was now resting on thin air.*

And going down.

Uuugghhh. . . .

As she accelerated, she felt her stomach rise nearly to her throat. Given her target's head start, it was now moving slightly faster than she was. Two stories below *and holding.*

The next four seconds would turn out to be the longest in Tiffany Meyer's life.

As a young girl, she had had a recurring dream that she was Alice, chasing a rabbit into its hole at the base of a big old oak tree. To her surprise, she fell into what seemed to be a bottomless pit. Falling. Waiting to meet bottom. But she always woke up before she reached it.

But this was *no dream.*

She was quite a sight. Long legs extended, eyes fixed on the target she was *desperately* chasing. Her long, silky hair billowing high over her head. Eyes bulging. Teeth clenched. Arms waving like a hummingbird in flight.

The sides of the shaft were a complete blur, but she had a clear fix on the car below. She needed a flat place to land and something to grab on to.

She was catching up now. It actually looked as though the car was coming up at her.

By now she had fallen eight floors, but she still had *one* between her and her target.

The top of the car had a nasty looking set of gears on the right, but the middle seemed pretty clear. She'd hit that, then try to roll to the left and grab the escape door.

Bounce. . . . Bounce off the top. She had to keep from *bouncing off the top.*

Tiffany's mind flashed right through the two days and $10,000 she had invested in jump school 3 years before. Never thought it'd pay off in a damn elevator shaft.

Go limp. Go limp and *roll* on impact. Roll? Roll where???? To the left—*just* a little bit. *Please!!!*

She would hit after falling a total of 10 floors. Because she was landing on an object that was falling itself, the net impact would be that of a 2½-story fall.

Tiffany Meyer was about to find out *why people are afraid of heights.*

Her right foot hit its target slightly before her left. If her right knee had been bent just a little, the shinbone would have survived the impact. But the knee was locked. In the split second that her upper body leveled its full force on the leg, the bone snapped. There was no support from her broken right leg. The left, however, landed bent and intact.

With some support from the left and none from the right, her roll would be in the *wrong* direction.

To the right—*in the direction of the gears.*

There were three of them. The largest had 3-inch teeth. Tiffany's right shoulder hit the next smaller size—the 2 inchers. The teeth weren't sharp but they *did* have a blunt edge. At impact, it easily ripped through her wool jacket and silk blouse, gouging out 4 inches of flesh and muscle from her shoulder.

Tiffany got no message from her shoulder, but the pain in her right leg was *searing*. The gears were about a foot from the edge of the car. As she rolled from her right shoulder, her left found that edge, *but it didn't catch.*

Going over the side. She could feel it. The Needle was going to win.

And she was going to die. . . .

In desperation, Tiffany slammed her right arm down, grabbing for *anything.* Desperate moves sometimes pay off. *This one did.* Her wrist locked between the teeth of the largest gear. It held!

Her right wrist was at the top of the car. But the rest of her dangled—from elbow to toe.

And now the true meaning of *PAIN.*

Her entire right arm was on fire. The shoulder was coming in loud and clear now. But the center of her agony was the "lucky" wrist locked in the gear.

But the pain was only beginning, for the car was beginning to *slow down* for its next stop.

Inside the elevator, the two passengers felt the sensation of a 25% increase in their body weights as the car began to decelerate in preparation for its stop. Outside, Tiffany felt as though a 30-pound weight had been attached to her dangling foot.

Thirty more pounds of pressure on that wrist.

Bones in a human hand are not very strong. The added pressure, as well as the elevator's tacking vibrations, helped the edge of the gear cut through her flesh and grind away at her naked wrist bones. She couldn't feel it happening through the pain, but *she was slipping.*

Tiffany was fighting a blackout. She *had* to do something to relieve the pain. She *had* to find a foothold.

Sliding her good leg along the wall of the car, she found what she was looking for—a seam separating two plates big enough for a toehold. This gave her the leverage to reach up and grab the gear with her left hand.

Just in time. Her right hand came free.

It was bloody, and it was numb, but it still functioned. She grabbed the gear with both hands, and pulled up far enough to get a knee-hold at the top of the car. As the car pulled to a stop, she climbed aboard.

Holding on to the top of that car for dear life, she didn't move as it renewed its journey downward. A tear rolled down her cheek, and dropped, mixing with the blood on the top of the car.

A *single* tear.

Two stops later, Tiffany found the strength to lift herself to a sitting position and peek through the escape door. Empty.

She lowered herself through the door, hanging by her hands from the top. By bending her broken leg, she was able to drop the 2 feet to the floor without further damage.

Then she crawled to the buttons, and hit LOBBY for the second time.

This time she got what she wanted.

When the doors opened at the lobby level, a shocked Jed Hirsch rushed to assist his boss, lying in a pool of blood on the floor of the elevator.

"Oh my God, Tiffany. *What have they done to you?*"

"*It's this damn building, Jed.* . . . But never mind. They're going to *kill* Bill. You've *got* to warn him. And get *me* out of here fast."

Jed wrapped his blue trench coat over her body to conceal the blood. He stooped down, pulled her up, and gently laid her body across his arms.

Fortunately, Bellow and crew had assumed Tiffany was safely incarcerated between 84 and 85. The security desk had not been alerted of a problem. Passing through, Jed told them that his companion was very ill and asked them to summon an ambulance. They did, but he did not wait for it.

Instead, he carried Tiffany down the escalator and onto the street. There he flagged a cab, and they proceeded to make their way around to the other side of Central Park.

But, traffic was crawling.

"Jed, there's *no time.* You've got to cross the park on foot to warn Bill. *Get him to the police as fast as you can.*"

"You've got it, Tiff."

Hirsch opened the door and scrambled out. Dodging traffic, he reached the park side of the street. The rally was about a half-mile away. He could hear the crowd.

Hirsch's wingtips were no substitute for track shoes, but he was about to top his best high-school track speed for the half-mile nonetheless. He flew past the zoo and under the bridge. The rally was now in sight. *But Bill Wilder wasn't.*

Jed made it to the edge of the crowd. People were disbursing. The rally was apparently over. Still no Wilder.

Then he spotted him. Bill was getting into his town car about 80 yards away.

Hirsch: "*BILL WILDER . . . STOP!*"

Incredibly, Wilder heard him. He turned, waved, but then proceeded to get into the car. Hirsch gave a warning signal to his driver.

Suddenly the car e x p   l   o   d   e   d!!!

The shock wave knocked Hirsch completely off his feet and onto his back. Pieces of debris flew hundreds of yards into the air. As he regained consciousness, Hirsch could hear the heavy items falling about him. He rolled over onto his stomach and covered his head with his hands. The bumper from the town car landed with a crash right next to him.

Jed's ears were ringing, but he could still hear cries of human anguish. He briefly thought of Bill Wilder, *but the sounds did not come from his former boss.* Jed lifted his head cautiously. The moans of anguish briefly stopped, and the world around him fell to a shocked silence.

Dust filled the air. Small pieces of carpeting, upholstery, clothing, and dust were settling to the ground. Hirsch struggled to his feet, and swept pieces of debris from his clothing.

He had been lucky. Twenty-four people who were within 50 yards of the car had been severely injured; 14 others had been killed. The scene resembled a battlefield, with broken bodies strewn in all directions.

Except for its engine and frame, the town car had literally disappeared. The engine was on fire. A column of thick, black smoke rose high above it.

It was over. The *whole thing* was over. . . . Just like that. . . .

Trembling, Hirsch wiped tears from his eyes. He headed back toward the street. He had to find Tiffany. . . . He had to get her to a hospital. . . . He had to get to her before *they* did.

EPILOGUE

"I, John Sanders, solemnly swear to protect, support, and defend the constitution of the United States of. . . ." It was January 20th, inauguration day for the Democratic candidate for president of the United States.

Tiffany Meyer was among the 110,523 to witness the historic event. The icy wind whipped through her hair. As usual, her injured right shoulder wasn't getting along very well with her crutches. But her doctor had assured her that, within 6 months, she'd be as good as new.

The cold wind brought tears to her eyes, momentarily blurring her vision. In spite of this, she was still able to make out the distinctive features of a diminutive figure, standing directly to the left of the outgoing president on the inauguration platform.

It was Brighton Bellow.

Brighton Bellow, once again presiding over the transfer of political power in the greatest country in the world. Sanders wasn't exactly his first choice. Bellow would have much preferred the Republican candidate. But Sanders would do nicely, thank you.

There *would* be a congressional investigation of the assassination of Bill Wilder. But Tiffany knew that Bellow, once again, had been dealt a pat hand.

No one really took her story seriously. Tiffany thought that the police, including the FBI, had been uncharacteristically superficial in their investigation. Basically, it came down to her word against *theirs.* There was absolutely no link that she, or anyone else, could establish between B&H and the powerful bomb that had been placed under the car, apparently while Bill had been speaking.

The dirty parts of the job had apparently been taken care of by organized crime. Bellow's power was indeed pervasive. He seemingly also controlled the important elements of the underground sectors of the economy as well as those on the surface.

We have a new President. He will rid us of the deficit by raising our taxes.

Then he will preside over the Second Great Depression.

Hail to the people.

POWER to the Chief.

Notes

1. See D. Clark, "Anxiety States: Panic and Generalized Anxiety," in *Cognitive Behavior Therapy for Psychiatric Problems: A Practical Guide,* K. Hawton et al., eds. (Oxford, England: Oxford University Press, 1989), pp. 52–96.
2. See P. Temin, *Did Monetary Forces Cause the Great Depression?* (New York: W. W. Norton, 1976).
3. C. Romer, "The Great Crash and the Onset of the Great Depression," 1990, *Quarterly Journal of Economics,* pp. 597–624. *See also* G. Bittlingmayer, "Output, Stock Volatility, and Political Uncertainty in a Natural Experiment: Germany, 1880–1940," working paper, Graduate School of Management, University of California, Davis, April 1997.

PART III

Solutions

SYNTHESIS

The Synthesis of Mysteries One through Five

The Three Components of Volatility

Professor Mayer *almost* got it right! There *are* multiple components to stock volatility. But there are *three*. Not two.

In an efficient market, there would be only one—the volatility related to changing general economic conditions, changes in firm prospects for generating future cash flows, tempered by the nature of the claims standing ahead of the equity stake in the firm's capital structure. Accurate responses to real-world events.

Call this *event-driven volatility*.

If event-driven volatility were the whole story, Shiller wouldn't have found the market's volatility to be excessive relative to the cash flows produced by firms.

But event-driven volatility is only a *small part* of the whole story.

An inefficient market makes mistakes. It overreacts to some events and underreacts to others. And the magnitude of the mis-reactions is *time-varying,* creating a *second* component of volatility.[1]—time-varying mistakes in pricing, relative to the receipt of new information.

Call this second component *error-driven volatility.*[2]

But this, too, is only a part of the whole story—and, I believe, only a *small* part. If the market merely reacts improperly to information coming in from the real world, why is the market's volatility so much smaller when the exchange is closed? After all, opinions about the impact of information received after the closing bell should be as misconceived as opinions formed when stocks are being traded.

Error-driven volatility should continue after the bell.

And we know that volatility is *much* different after the bell than when shares are being traded.

Our best estimate of the relative magnitudes of the market's volatility when open and when closed comes from French and Roll's measurements during exchange holidays. Here, we can be sure that the amount of real-world information coming on the exchange holiday is pretty much the same as on any other trading weekday. When we compare these holidays with other weekdays, we conclude that the variance of return is 25 times greater when the exchange is open. Because the volatility is the square root of the variance, this means the total volatility is 5 times greater.

Think about it. Only one source of information was shut down during exchange holidays.

The behavior of market prices.

I believe many investors are very interested in the minute-to-minute, hour-to-hour, and day-to-day changes taking place in stock market prices. I think investors are very concerned, not only about changes in the prices of the stocks they own, but also about changes that have taken place in the prices of other stocks *and in the market index.* I think there are sequences of past price changes that can induce investors to buy or sell *now.* Past price changes may serve as signals that induce trading, *creating* contemporary price changes.

This is why it is difficult to connect major price changes to major economic and world events. Most of the price changes aren't caused by real-world events; they're causally related, instead, to the market's own pricing behavior in the recent past.

This is why changes in fundamental economic and financial variables explain such a pathetically small fraction of the market's movement. For the most part, the market isn't driven by weather or by changes in fundamental variables; it is driven, instead, by changes in its own prices.

Current price reactions to past price changes constitute a third component of stock volatility. And it is, by far, the most important part.

This is THE BEAST.

We shall call the critical third component *price-driven volatility.* Price-driven volatility stops when trading stops. Of the three components, *it is the only one that stops.* And when it stops, total volatility drops by at least three-quarters,[3] making price-driven volatility *three times* as large as the other two components combined!

For cross-listed stocks, the length of the trading day and the quantity of information that the market is reacting to becomes larger. The volume of trading on the LSE for the cross-listed stocks is less than on the NYSE, so we don't see a doubling of total volatility, but we see a significant increase just the same.

Price-Driven Volatility Is Unstable
Of the three components, price-driven volatility is likely to be the least stable.

For the well-diversified market index, there is likely to be considerable time-diversification in the appearance of economic events like earnings reports, the release of macroeconomic numbers, etc. Moreover, we can expect that the markets tendencies to overreact to some of these numbers and underreact to others will evolve slowly over time. Thus, it is unlikely that we will see sudden and frequent changes in either event-driven or error-driven volatility.

We know that *total* volatility, the *combination* of the three individual volatilities, does, in fact, change *suddenly* and *frequently,* so the instability is likely to be coming from *price-driven* volatility. It is not unlikely that, given the nature of the complex process by which the market reacts to its own price history, a particular sequence, or configuration, of price changes may trigger successive price reactions that eventually build into a volatility increase or decrease.

To an investor, price-driven volatility is as real, and as painful, as either of the other two components.

Investors don't like volatility—any kind of volatility. When they realize that volatility has increased, they react to it by driving prices down. And the very fall in prices becomes part of the technical history that may yield further price adjustments.

How do investors come to realize that there has been a change in the level of price-driven volatility. By watching the pricing process and *learning*. Watching the sequence of price changes they, as traders, are generating.

In the four days before October 16, 1987, there were three percentage price changes that were multiple standard-deviation events.[4] Then came the truly large drop on Friday. Four multiple standard-deviation events in 5 days. Of course, the likelihood that these four events came from the former distribution of possible price changes is remote.

Time for a dramatic revision in the market's estimate of its own price-driven volatility. And this revision in beliefs itself called for another price adjustment at the opening bell on Monday, the 19th. And *this* 200-point reaction after the opening bell called for a further revision of the volatility estimate and a still further price reaction by the highly risk-averse market.

The market is capable of driving itself right into the ground! *Price reactions that feed on themselves*—this is the nature of price-driven volatility. This is the nature of *THE BEAST.*

Price-driven volatility is real, and investors are very much afraid of it. They *should be.*

It's systematic and nondiversifiable.

Because investors focus their attention on changes in the value of the *market index.* They respond to signals from the market index and then take action by trading in individual issues, making the price changes associated with price-driven volatility correlate across the cross-section of stocks.

The Synthesis of the Sixth Mystery

We have seen that firms that recapitalize, by exchanging bonds for stock, experience a significant reduction in their overall risk. Kaplan and Stein find that, after, increasing the amount of debt on average from 25% to 81% of total capital claims, including equity, the beta factors of the equity in their firms went from an average of 1.01 to 1.38. In the absence of any other change, KS would have expected the equity betas to average more than 4.00.

What happened?

As the October 19th experience clearly shows, the price changes associated with price-driven volatility are likely to be correlated across different stocks. Because the returns associated with price-driven volatility are correlated stock to stock, price-driven volatility becomes an important part of a stock's market beta factor. Beta can be broken into two components—a component related to (a) correlated—across different stocks—price reactions and misreactions to real-world news and (b) price reactions to the technical price history. The first component reflects event-driven and error-driven volatility and the second, price-driven volatility.

Because event-driven and error-driven volatility stem from events that change either discount rates or prospects for future cash flows, the beta component related to these two volatilities will increase proportionately with financial leverage. Indeed, their preconception of an efficient market led KS to their expectation that the leveraged equity betas should average in excess of 4.00.

But what if the price-driven component is the truly dominant part of a stock's beta?

There is *no* reason to believe that price reactions to the *changing nature of a stock's technical pricing history* will increase in absolute value as the amount of debt in a firm's capital structure becomes larger.

Once we realize that the lion's share of KS's original beta of 1.01 was related mostly to price-driven volatility, which is unaffected by the amount of debt employed in financing, the modest increase in beta to 1.38 rather than 4.00 should not come as a surprise.

There is another way of looking at what happened. Same essential explanation. Different words.

Bonds are fixed-income securities. The *defined* income stream may provide an anchor for pricing by bond investors. With their *residual* claim, common stocks have no such anchor. Stock investors may have a greater propensity to trade on the basis of the technical history of the price than on the changing prospects for the long-term stream of expected future dividends.

After all, the stock market is populated by many technical chartists of various types, but fewer of these people populate the bond market. In fact, many in the stock market (except those who invest exclusively in indexes) engage in some form of timing (stocks vs. bonds, sectors, industries, and even individual stocks) with respect to their investments. As price-driven volatility increases, the relative rankings of these investments are shuffled, leading to trades in portfolios. In this sense, volatility is a primary driver of trading stocks.

Suppose price-driven volatility is significantly *lower* in the bond market. This being the case, if a firm goes from a situation where fully 75% of its claims are traded in the relatively noisy stock market to one where only 19% of its claims are subject to the *loud* noise of price-driven volatility, why should we be surprised to see the total risk associated with *all* its claims fall dramatically?

Keep in mind that, in all seven mysteries, we are dealing with *very high magnitude anomalies*. The magnitudes of those numbers are very much consistent with the dramatic drop in asset risk observed by Kaplan and Stein.

Synthesis of the Seventh Mystery

Why Closed-End Funds Sell at Discounts

Why do closed-end investment companies sell at discounts? I believe Lee, Shleifer, and Thaler got it right, when they conjectured that, because of the time-varying nature of the discounts, risk-averse investors discount the prices of closed-end funds to provide themselves with higher future expected rates of return.

Those who directly buy the stocks owned by the closed-end fund get a heavy dose of price-driven volatility. But those who buy the fund get a second dose on top of that—the price, and through the price, the discount of the closed-end fund reacting to *its own* technical price history.

Fortunately, the market value of the investments in the fund is published weekly, and that serves as an anchor for the market's pricing. But funds usually sell at discounts even on the days their underlying market values become known, and the magnitudes of the discounts, even on these days, varies *considerably* over time. Buy a closed-end fund and you must eat a second dose of price-driven volatility.

Thus, we have a rationale for the discount being there *on average*. But given the strong price-driven volatility, funds can also sell at premiums from time to time.

If the discount is shrinking, the market may project a continuation of the trend and drive the price of the fund to even higher levels. Thus, price-driven volatility creates considerable cross-sectional variation in the magnitudes of the discounts, and it may even create premiums for a few funds.

Why Changes in the Discounts Are Negatively Related to Stock Returns

Take another look at Figure 1.11 in Part I. This figure tells us that an increase in the magnitude of the discount is associated with lower stock returns. Why? First, the source of the discounts is price-driven volatility. And price-driven volatility is unstable.

We can expect an *increase* in price-driven volatility to have two simultaneous effects. First, it will make risk-averse investors require higher rates of return on their stock investments. Based on the works of (a) Haugen, Talmor, and Torous; (b) French, Schwert and Stambaugh;[5] and (c) Cutler, Poterba, and Summers, we can expect a negative price adjustment and a temporary period of low returns on stocks *in general*.

Second, since the discounts on the closed-end funds are related to the magnitude of price-driven volatility, they should become larger as the returns to stocks become smaller, as the market gears up for higher future returns to compensate for greater volatility.

But why is the relationship between the discounts and stock returns more pronounced for smaller firms? The case for greater price-driven volatility in small stocks can be made using the results of French and Roll. Recall, from Table 1.6, that the difference between exchange-open and exchange-closed combined volatility is *much bigger* for small firms than it is for large ones.

The evidence suggests that smaller firms simply have greater price-driven volatility, and accordingly, are likely to experience larger changes in this volatility. So as the closed-end discounts become larger in response to an increase in price-driven volatility, the returns to the smaller firms can be expected to fall further.

Seven mysteries resolved in one stroke—once we recognize the presence of very high levels of price-driven volatility.

IMPLICATIONS

The Implications for Corporate Finance

Investment and the Relative Allocation of Capital to Different Firms

In a capitalistic economy, markets ultimately determine *what* is produced, *who* produces it, and *how* it is produced. These decisions are made as people vote with their incomes and wealth in the market for goods and services, in the market for land, in the market for labor, and, importantly, *in the market for capital.*

Firms raise capital by issuing securities and, if capital is to flow to its highest and best use, the prices of those securities must accurately reflect the efficiency by which the goods and services are to be produced, the risk undertaken in their production, and the quality and desirability of the goods and services in satisfying consumer demand.

Price-driven volatility can muck this whole process up *pretty badly.* If two-thirds of a stock's price fluctuations are purely related to price behavior, market prices and underlying intrinsic values—while ultimately connected in the long run—may be all but unconnected in the short term.

Intrinsic value is the best estimate of the price of the stock, taking into account all information relevant to projecting the expected values of the future cash flows as well as the risk associated with producing these flows. If market prices were always equal to intrinsic values, we would have an efficient market. The market would send capital to its highest and best use, even in the short term. And if market prices were always equal to intrinsic values, we would have only event-driven volatility.

Error-driven and price-driven volatility are *spoilers* in this process. To see how, consider Figures 3.1, 3.2, and 3.3. In the figures, we plot the intrinsic value of each stock on the horizontal axis and its market price on the vertical axis. Figures 3.1 and 3.2 show the respective values at a single point in time. Figure 3.1 is an efficient market, where market prices and intrinsic values are always the same.

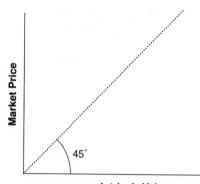

Market Price

Intrinsic Value

FIGURE 3.1 Efficient Market at One Point in Time

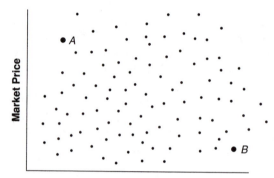

Market Price

● A

● B

Intrinsic Value

FIGURE 3.2 Actual Market at One Point in Time

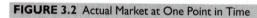

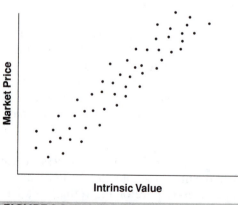

Market Price

Intrinsic Value

FIGURE 3.3 Actual Market (Average over N Years)

The market of Figure 3.2 is consistent with the evidence presented in this book. Here, while there is a very loose relationship between prices and intrinsic values, there are many under- and over-valued firms.

Take the firm labeled "*A*" for example. By some combination of "improper" reactions to (a) real-world events and (b) signals coming from the market's technical history, the stock has become grossly overpriced. The company's management probably knows this. They know that they can raise capital by selling stock at very cheap expected rates of return. If they earn, on their investments, rates of profit that exceed the cheap rate of return on the stock they issue, they increase the wealth of their current stockholders. So they make investments that would otherwise be rejected as insufficiently profitable.

They overinvest. They build plant and equipment to produce products that are either too costly relative to close substitutes or simply not in great demand by consumers. Consumers *get* what they *don't want.*

They may really *want* the product that's sitting on the drawing board of the firm labeled "*B*" in Figure 3.2. However, this firm's stock is grossly *undervalued.* It *would* invest to produce the product that consumers really want, if it could raise capital at a fair price, but in this market, it can't.

Thus, the error-driven and price-driven volatilities affect the *relative* allocation of capital between firms, rendering the ultimate menu of goods and services produced *suboptimal.*

In the long run, market prices are likely to gravitate toward their intrinsic values. Figure 3.3 plots *n*-year average market prices against *n*-year average intrinsic values. On average, these firms will be investing optimal amounts.

We should take little comfort in this, however, because, during the *n*-year period, individual firms will be overinvesting when they are in the northwest half of the graph and underinvesting when they are in the southeast.

But take *some* comfort. At least *on average,* the capital market will be getting it right!

How long is "*n*"? The number of years it takes to average to a cluster like that of Figure 3.3 depends on the relative magnitudes of error-driven and price-driven volatility. If they are truly dominant, which the evidence would seem to indicate, *n* is a long, long time.

But as bad as this is, it isn't the real problem. *The real problem is that stock volatility has been, and is, devouring big chunks of our wealth!*

General Underinvestment

Thus, the error-driven and price-driven volatilities create distortions in the *relative* allocation of capital to producers. However, as a general rule, they *also* cause firms to *underinvest*.

The cost of equity capital is comprised of a risk-free rate and a risk premium. In an efficient capital market, the risk premium accurately reflects the risks associated with the management of the firm and the production and distribution of products.

Error-driven and, especially, price-driven volatility present investors with a truly major source of additional risk, which dramatically increases the size of the risk premium and the return investors require on investments financed through equity capital. Because of this, firms will forgo investments they would have made in the absence of error-driven and price-driven volatility.

I have argued that the variance of stock returns is 16 times as large as it would be without price-driven volatility. Under reasonable assumptions, one can argue that the risk premium on equities is proportional to the variance. Given this, the equity risk premium is 16 times larger than it needs to be! Over the twentieth century the real, inflation-adjusted, realized equity risk premium has averaged about 6%. The real, risk-free rate has averaged about 1%. Thus, the real total return to stocks has averaged about 7%. Without price-driven volatility, the risk premium arguably would have been only .4%, making the total real return to equity only 1.4%. This implies that the real cost of equity capital has been *5 times higher than it needs to be.*

For those who feel that this conjecture is incredible, stop and think. *This conclusion is consistent with all of the evidence presented in Part I.*

And the implications are *enormous!*

Price-driven volatility has greatly inhibited investment spending over the years. Ultimately, it has acted, and acts, as a serious drag on economic growth in this country and around the world. We lose sight of its significance because it has been with us since we started trading stocks under the tree in New York City. If you drag a ball and chain around for your entire life, you will likely become accustomed to and, therefore, miss the significance of its burden.

This will be especially true if everyone you know also has a ball and chain. Because the rules of trading are similar in the major stock markets of the world, all are probably plagued by heavy doses of price-driven volatility.

It's difficult for us to comprehend a world *without* price-driven volatility. It is pervasive—always and everywhere! And as we move steadily toward a 24-hour trading day, things are going to get much worse.

Astonishingly, we can easily get rid of our ball and chain. Below, I discuss the possibility of an instantaneous daily auction, where trades are crossed and where the average crossed prices for stocks are reported. In such a framework, price-driven volatility is reduced dramatically. We now have the computational capacity to trade this way.

In their study of market volatility during nontrading hours, French and Roll stumbled on arguably the most important discovery in the history of modern finance. *During what would have been the normal trading hours on the exchange holidays of 1968, the variance of stock returns was a mere 16th of its value during trading on regular days.* Unfortunately, their steadfast belief in efficient-markets dogma led them to reject the rather obvious implications of this revelation. They chose, instead, to explain their discovery by hypothesizing that professional investors stopped searching during these holidays simply because they were unable to trade immediately upon discovery—an explanation that an unindoctrinated person would, quite simply, find preposterous!

The Question of Optimal Capital Structure

Any MBA with an emphasis in finance knows the irrelevance theorems of Modigliani and Miller (MM).[6] Basically, the theorems state that, if the market is efficient and all types of securities are fairly priced, it makes no difference to the total value of your firm whether you issue debt or equity to finance your investments. If you sell bonds at a fair price, you will have made a fair deal with your new bondholders. Because the deal is fair, no wealth is transferred from or to bondholders or stockholders. The value of the firm is the same as if a new block of *stock* had been sold at a fair price.

Apparently, however, the market doesn't feel that way. I can say that because a professor named Masulis[7] studied the reaction of stock prices to exchange offers. In an exchange offer, the firm might ask its bondholders to exchange their bonds for shares of the firm's stock. If the majority of the bondholders agree to the terms of the offer, it is binding on all. The firm could also ask its stockholders to exchange bonds for a fraction of their stock. In either case, there is a change in the firm's capital structure, with no change in the composition of the firm's assets.

So an exchange offer gives us the opportunity to see the impact of a pure change in capital structure. Figure 3.4 shows the reaction of stock prices to the

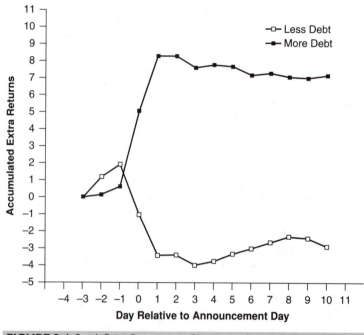

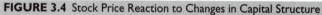

FIGURE 3.4 Stock Price Reaction to Changes in Capital Structure

Note: Adapted from Masulis, R., "The Effects of Capital Structure Change on Security Prices: A Study of Exchange Offers," *Journal of Financial Economics,* 1980, June, pp. 139–177.

announcement of exchange offers of both types. The unfilled squares show the daily cumulative return to the firm's stock in the days surrounding an announcement of a trade of stock for debt. The filled squares show the reaction to debt for stock. A clear dichotomy. The value of the firm goes up with more debt and down with less.

Modern finance offers several explanations for these reactions. They are, of course, based on rational human behavior.

The first explanation is based on taxes. The interest payments to the bondholders are deductible. Dividend payments to stockholders are not.

In this context, there are three claims to the corporate pie—stockholders, bondholders, and the Internal Revenue Service. If we issue more debt, we increase the firm's tax shield, reducing the IRS's share of the pie, while keeping the total size of the pie intact. The aggregate size of the shares going to bondholders and stockholders increases. Thus, the increase in the stock price seen in Figure 3.4 may reflect the squeeze put on the IRS.

Modern finance's other explanation is that the interest payments on the new debt raise the bar management must jump over to avoid bankruptcy. If investors believe management is really concerned about bankruptcy, they may raise their opinion about the *size* of the corporate pie. Management, after all, has "put their money where their mouth is." If they didn't believe they could jump over the higher bar, they wouldn't have raised it! In the case of equity for debt, management is lowering the bar, so "maybe they're not as confident as we thought they were."

Under this explanation the reactions to the announcement are the result of changing market expectations about the profitability of the firm.[8]

Now we have a third explanation.

Suppose there is much more price-driven volatility in the stock market than in the bond market. As the firm trades debt for equity, a larger fraction of its securities will be traded in a less noisy market. As we saw in the study by Kaplan and Stein, the overall risk of the firm will fall. Its average cost of capital will go down and its value will rise. The opposite happens when stock is exchanged for debt. The reactions shown in Figure 3.4 may reflect the expectation of significant increases and decreases in the risk of the firm.[9]

High levels of price-driven volatility in the stock market create a clear incentive for management to lean in the direction of debt in financing their investments.[10]

Implications for Investors

I'm sorry. Given the present rules and regulations, investors will just have to live with price-driven volatility.

But its instability is intriguing. Can we predict volatility bursts and thereby avoid getting caught in a stock market crash?

Unfortunately, a major volatility burst is strikingly similar to an earthquake:

- Plot the daily percentage changes in stock prices during a volatility burst and it looks very much like tremors plotted on a seismograph.
- Like an earthquake, the market's tremors usually dissipate after a while.
- If the volatility bust is big enough, you may see "aftershocks."[11]
- Both are scary as hell.
- Neither is very predictable

Volatility bursts come suddenly and unpredictably. If you try to predict them, you can count on many false alarms. So many, in fact, that you may quickly grow tired of "burst prediction." But at least now you can understand *what* is happening *while* it is happening.

During really major volatility bursts, I frequently get calls from the media asking for an explanation for the stock market's strange behavior. In the case of 1987, they seemed to want to pin it on the federal deficit.

It was as though they thought that the market had suddenly caught on to the fact that the government had been running deficits for all those years.

Nonsense.

The market was just going through a process of "scaring *itself* to death." It had done that many times before, and it will do it many times again. The key thing to watch for is the *dissipation* of the price-driven volatility. If it goes away, things will be fine. And if it doesn't. . . .

Another interesting implication of price-driven volatility is the status of illiquid investments like real estate. In making their asset allocation decisions, pension funds usually assign a relatively low rate of return to real estate investments as an asset class. This may seem strange to some, because the risk associated with the cash flows produced by real estate investments in ventures like shopping malls and office buildings isn't unlike the risk associated with most corporate investments. Yet, real estate is usually assigned a much lower expected return than common stock in the asset allocation problem.

Real estate is not actively traded. It has little or no price-driven volatility. But as we now know, price-driven volatility plays a major role in the risk of common stock investments, as well as a major role in the formation of the equity risk premium on stock. The risk premium for real estate *should* be much smaller.

Some real estate investments are traded on the NYSE. These investments are closed-end investment companies, called real estate investment trusts (REITs).

They are liquid investments; ordinary real estate is not. Ordinary real estate did not crash in October of 1987, but REITs *did!*

Policy Implications

Price-Driven Volatility and the Nature of the Marketplace

Price-driven volatility is created in the capital marketplace. Its stability and magnitude are, therefore, related to the rules and practices of the capital marketplace. The length of the trading day. The speed with which trades are processed. The extent to which trades are executed on crossing networks like SCARE. The existence of derivative securities like futures and options contracts. The use of program trading. The nature of the array of execution alternatives like market and stop-loss orders. The presence of rules that shut down markets after experiencing daily price changes over a given limit. The extent to which stocks are cross-listed. And the extent to which the media communicates what's going on in the marketplace to the general population.

Change the nature of the trading process, and you will probably change the level of price-driven volatility.

And remember, based on all the evidence presented in this book, we can say that price-driven volatility *dominates.*

Changes in the nature of the trading environment should be taken much more seriously than they are presently.

The Length of the Trading Day
For quite some time, stocks have traded during nonholiday weekdays for a 6½-hour period. If anything, this period should be *reduced,* not extended. Trades can now be processed, using powerful computers, at extremely high rates of speed. With processing power increasing at a faster rate than trading volume, we should be able to process the current volume of trades in shorter periods of time.

Let's pause to distinguish between clock time and trading time. Clock time is measured in minutes and seconds. Trading time is measured in the number of trades executed. There is usually a fixed amount of clock time in a given trading day—6½ hours. However, the amount of *trading* time varies enormously from day to day.

We know that price-driven volatility increases directly with the amount of clock time in a given trading day. But, given the clock time expired, does price-driven volatility increase proportionately with trading time? Possibly, but remember that price-driven volatility feeds on *observed* price changes.

Think of an alternative way of trading stock. An instantaneous auction. Before the auction, demanders submit prices and amounts they are willing to buy at the different prices. Suppliers would do the same thing for quantities of stock they are willing to sell at different prices. Orders are prioritized based on time of submission. At the end of the auction, prices will be reported for each stock at the volume-weighted average traded price for the day.

In this market, investors will likely act on the net price changes that occur from one auction to the next. My guess is that they wouldn't put much weight on what happened *inside* the auction period. Price-driven volatility probably wouldn't be affected by the number of trades processed either.

To preserve liquidity, we need to accommodate all buyers and sellers who desire to participate in the stock market, say at the beginning of any given trading day. But how much do we gain by allowing continuous access to the market over extended periods of clock time? Why not merely process the daily inventory of desired trades via crossing networks and computers, report the net price changes, and then wait for the next day's round?

We'd have a cost and a benefit associated with truncating the trading day in this way. The cost is a small loss in market liquidity. The benefit is a large potential decline in price-driven volatility.[12]

Lower technical volatility would increase the market's efficiency in properly allocating capital to different firms. It would also result in a general reduction in the cost of capital across all firms, resulting in a stimulation of investment spending, increased production by corporations, and real gains in economic growth.

We should think through the benefits and costs associated with cross-listing stocks in a similar manner.

Circuit Breakers

Following the 1987 crash, the Presidential Task Force on Market Mechanisms recommended the establishment of "circuit breakers" in which trading would temporarily cease following market moves of a given magnitude.

Given the experience of October 19, circuit breakers would seem to be a good idea. However, given how little we know about the market's learning process, in which price changes feed into others, it's difficult to say just how beneficial circuit breakers are.

Advocates of market efficiency have problems with circuit breakers. Grossman,[13] for example, has stated that the closing of markets "merely prevents consenting adults from carrying out their desires on the floor of the stock exchange." However, one can make a similar statement about prohibitions against rioting at a British soccer game. Riotous behavior is clearly destructive and against the interest of established society. But what about the chaos that sometimes occurs on the floor of the New York Stock Exchange? Ultimately, whose interests does it serve?

Circuit breakers are designed to control price-driven volatility. Advocates of efficient markets don't believe price-driven volatility exists. Therefore, there is no place in their world for circuit breakers.

But we now know that price-driven volatility *does* exist. Big time! Price-driven volatility feeds on information produced by price changes. Stop the price changes and you starve price-driven volatility.

Circuit breakers act to shorten the length of the trading day during periods of turmoil in the market.[14] Based on the evidence we've seen connecting the length of the trading day with the magnitude of price-driven volatility, *they should work.*

Trading Halts

Circuit breakers shut down trading across the entire exchange. Trading halts happen to stocks, individually.

Although stock exchanges in the United States follow a continuous auction process, when the market is put under severe stress, the specialist, who makes a market in a particular stock, may call for a temporary suspension in the continuous process.

An order imbalance halt occurs when the specialist receives an unusual flow of orders that can't be matched. Halts can also occur when unusually important announcements are pending. During a halt, the specialist engages in price exploration by issuing indicator quotes. These quotes set lower and upper bounds for reopening prices. Investors responding to indicator quotes get execution priority when the halt comes to an end.

It isn't clear that trading halts offer the same type of benefits as circuit breakers.

First, the media usually report trading halts. Media coverage can attract attention, which can lead to greater volatility. Circuit breakers are triggered by major market moves. The moves themselves have been much more important to the media than the triggering of the circuit breakers.

Second, empirical evidence[15] indicates that volatility is actually greater following a trading halt than it is in control periods matched on time of day, duration, and returns net of market returns.

Although there is no reason to suspect, from the evidence presented in this book, that trading halts are harmful, it doesn't seem that they help our problem very much.

FINAL WORDS

The merit of a scientific paradigm lies in its ability to *predict* the future or to *explain* what has happened in the past.

Modern finance started out with great promise in this regard. The earliest evidence was consistent with the notion that the changes in stock prices were random.

The Efficient Markets Hypothesis *was able to explain that.* Instantaneous price responses to the receipt of random and completely unpredictable information.

Very satisfying at the time.

But now we know that there are important *seasonal* patterns in returns. And Modern Finance cannot explain that.

And now we know that there are important short-term reversal, intermediate-term inertia, and long-term reversal patterns in stock returns. And Modern Finance cannot explain *that.*

We also know that stock portfolios of unambiguously lower risk have higher expected returns.[16]

And Modern Finance cannot explain that.

Just what *can* the paradigms of Modern Finance explain or predict about the stock market? To see, try to explain the differences in the total rates of return to stocks in a given month. Explain the differences by relating them to differences in the nature of the companies behind the stocks. Which of the stocks are the most profitable? Which have the most debt? Which are the largest? Which have the highest beta factors?

You will find that many of these factors are statistically significant in explaining the cross-section of differences in monthly returns. But none explain or predict in a manner consistent with the predictions of Modern Finance.

All owe their predictive power to *error-driven volatility.*

They predict well because they exploit the market's nature to misprice. To overreact to some types of information and underreact to others. They *predict* well in spite of the fact that factor models of this type are typically capable of explaining only 10% of the differences in returns across the stock population.

Only 10%!

What explains the remaining 90%? I believe that much of it will eventually be explained when we come to understand the complex mechanics of price-driven volatility.

But we will never come to understand *what we don't admit exists.*

Most of the profession remains focused on the *0%* of the differences explained by the paradigms of Modern Finance. The 10% related to error-driven volatility may be interesting to many of us, but the real challenge lies within the remaining 90%.

There is much work to be done.

In fact,

we haven't really started!

Have we?

Notes

1. If the market is slow to react to important pieces of information, it is possible that the error-driven component could be *negative.*
2. Factor models that successfully explain and predict differences in the rates of return to stocks owe their predictive and explanatory power to the presence of *reactive volatility.* See, for example, R. Haugen and N. Baker, 1996, "Commonality in the Determinants of Expected Stock Returns," *Journal of Financial Economics,* pp. 401–439.
3. French and Roll's results indicate that because the variance across the Wednesday exchange holiday and the following Thursday is only 1.145 times as great as on single weekdays, the variance is 25 times as great, on average, in the hours the market is open than in the average of *all* hours when the market is closed. All non-trading hours are, of course, not equal when it comes to the arrival of new information from the real world. What we are really interested in is the market's volatility during the hours between 9:30 A.M. and 3:30 P.M. *during the exchange holiday,* as compared to the same hours of the day on other weekdays when the exchange is open. Assuming the aggregate of event-driven and error-driven *variance* is half as large, on average, during the other closed hours as it was for the holiday from 9:30 A.M. to 3:30 P.M., we can still say that total variance is roughly 15 times as large (and the volatility nearly four times as large) when the exchange was open on other weekdays between 9:30 A.M. and 3:30 P.M. than when it was closed *during these hours* on exchange holidays.
4. Based on the implied volatility of the market index as computed from the relative prices of S&P 100 index options and the value for the index itself.
5. See footnote 1 in part I.
6. See F. Modigliani and M. Miller, 1958, "The Cost of Capital, Corporation Finance, and the Theory of the Firm," *American Economic Review,* pp. 261–297.
7. See R. Masulis, 1980, "The Effects of Capital Structure Change on Security Prices: A Study of Exchange Offers," *Journal of Financial Economics,* pp. 139–177.
8. There are some problems with both explanations. Miller, of Modigliani and Miller, argues that the interest rate on corporate debt is grossed up by corporations trying to take advantage of the tax shield, to the point that all tax savings actually go to bondholders in the form of higher interest rates. See M. Miller, 1977, "Debt and Taxes," *Journal of Finance,* pp. 261–275. Moreover, it's not clear whether management would consider bankruptcy to be a significant hurdle. After all, if things don't work out as expected, and bankruptcy becomes a problem,

management can easily eliminate the problem with another exchange offer—exchanging stock for bonds at fair market values. For a detailed discussion, see R. Haugen and L. Senbet, 1978, "The Insignificance of Bankruptcy Costs to the Theory of Optimal Capital Structure," *Journal of Finance,* pp. 383–393.

9. Kaplan and Stein report a 44% average cumulative excess return on their 12 stocks in the period extending 2 months before the recapitalization announcements to the completion of the transaction. Some of this reaction may be attributable to expected increases in efficiency following the recaps. However, a significant fraction of the premium may be in anticipation of the risk reduction, which Kaplan and Stein actually find.

10. As an aside, management should also seriously consider the implications of cross-listing on the risk of their firms.

11. For example, the burst occurring on October 13, 1989, may have been an aftershock of the burst associated with the 1987 crash.

12. The relationship between trading time and volatility is not likely to be linear. One interesting example that may point to nonlinearity is Poland. The Polish stock market is open for a relatively short period of time. Yet Polish stocks are highly volatile. This may indicate that short trading periods are sufficient to create large amounts of price-driven volatility. As a caveat, however, we should recognize that there is a great deal of uncertainty associated with the fledgling Polish economy. Moreover, Polish stocks are very thinly traded, and are subject to great price pressure from foreign investors who are moving large blocks of money into emerging markets.

13. See S. Grossman, 1990, "Introduction to the NBER Symposium on the 1987 Crash," *Review of Financial Studies,* pp. 1–3.

14. Perhaps, however, we need a better measure of "turmoil." Circuit breakers might work more efficiently if they were triggered by a measure of market volatility—such as the implied standard deviation embedded in the prices of stock index options.

15. See C. Lee, M. Ready, and P. Seguin, 1994, "Volume, Volatility and New York Stock Exchange Trading Halts," *Journal of Finance,* pp. 183–214.

16. Haugen and Baker find that the stock portfolios that produce the highest rates of return have low debt-to-equity ratios, low volatility of return, low betas, high liquidity, high market capitalization, and high rates of profitability and interest coverage. Companies with low expected return have the opposite profile.